the Only BOOK

Library of Congress Cataloging-in-Publication Data is available.
Visit the Random House Reference Web site at www.randomwords.com
Typeset and printed in the United States of America.
ISBN: 0-375-72027-8

0 9 8 7 6 5 4 3 2

GERARD & PATRICIA DEL RE

the Only BOOK

THE NEW AND ULTIMATE COMPENDIUM OF **ONE-OF-A-KIND FACTS**

Random House Reference
New York • Toronto • London • Sydney • Auckland

Introduction

The Only Book is a delightful storehouse of "only" facts on every subject—including music, movies, sports, science, religion, literature, and history. An "only" fact, of course, is a fact that is unique, one-of-a-kind, unduplicated, and not likely to be equaled. The "only" facts in this new and ultimate compendium are "onlys" that have withstood the test of time.

Leaf through the pages to find questions such as: *Name the only U.S. general to win a Nobel Peace Prize? What nation's constitution forbids maintaining military forces? Name the only celebrity to have been arrested on her deathbed. Who is the only woman buried among the popes at the Vatican? What is the only member of the cat family that is actually social by nature?* Answers under each question usually contain dates and other pertinent facts to give you the big picture.

The purpose of **The Only Book** is not to stump or present trick questions. Rather, its aim is to inform, enlighten, and stimulate the curiosity. The reader will come away from it with unique facts that can be shared with others. The "only" facts presented here are indeed trivia, but they're not trivial.

Gerard 🅔 Patricia Del Re

Table of Contents

Countries, Cities & States

Name the only country named after a tree.

Brazil is the only country named after a tree, the brazilwood. Brazilwood is a tropical redwood that yields a crimson, purple or pink dye and is often used to make cabinets and violin bows. Its name is derived from the East Indian redwood called "bresel wood." When sixteenth century Portuguese explorers came to South America, they encountered the similar-looking South American tree, named it brazilwood, and made a fortune selling fashionable red dyes to European manufacturers. They named the country Brazil in honor of the lucrative tree.

Where is the only freshwater lake to contain ocean fish such as sharks, swordfish, and tuna?

Lake Nicaragua in Nicaragua, Central America, is the largest lake in Central America. Lake Nicaragua's waters are rich in ocean fish stock, although the water is fresh. Scientists believe that the lake was once part of the Pacific until massive volcanic eruptions completely separated it and the saltwater animals evolved to live in a freshwater environment.

Name the only body of water in the world in which one is unable to swim and that is totally devoid of fish and plant life (not due to pollution).

The Dead Sea (also known as the Salt Sea), situated between Israel and Jordan, is the only body of water in the world in which one is unable to swim. Instead, one will float, due to briny water that is as thick as glue. No body of water anywhere is saltier. No fish or plant life, not even algae or insects, can live in what is actually a salt lake.

What is the only Central American country that doesn't border the Caribbean?

El Salvador is the only Central American country that doesn't border the Caribbean Sea.

What is the only nation over which the sun rises and sets at the same time?

The only nation on earth that is so vast that the sun rises and sets at the same time is Russia, which has eleven time zones.

Name the only country in the world where the sun can be observed rising in the Atlantic and setting in the Pacific.

The only country in the world where it's possible for one to observe the sun rising in the Atlantic Ocean and setting in the Pacific is Panama in Central America.

Name the only place in the world where a language officially known as Rock English is spoken.

Gibraltar, a crown colony of Great Britain, is the only place where Rock English is spoken. Rock English is a mixture of Spanish and English patois. Gibraltar is defined by its topography of solid rock and juts out into the Strait of Gibraltar (toward Morocco), which separates the Mediterranean from the Atlantic.

Name the only country that doesn't print its name on its stamps.

Great Britain is the only country that doesn't print its name on its stamps. Stamps from Great Britain usually feature a silhouette of the monarch's head.

What is the only foreign country that has a capital city named after an American President?

The capital of Liberia is Monrovia, named after U.S. President James Monroe. Monrovia was founded by freed American slaves in 1822, and named after the American President of the time.

What is the only major river that flows both north and south of the equator?

The only major river that flows on both sides of the equator is the Congo, which flows through the Republic of the Congo, the Democratic Republic of the Congo, and Angola. It crosses the equator twice.

Can you name the only country in
the world that attracts ten million tourists
annually but has no hotels, motels,
restaurants, nightclubs, movie houses,
taverns, or drugstores?

Vatican City, or the Holy See, renowned for its great works of art
and architecture, is the only country in the world that has no such
accommodations. Visitors must leave Vatican City and enter the city
of Rome, Italy, for food, lodging, and other services. Visitors come to
Vatican city to enjoy the art, see the Pope's home, and reflect.

What is the only South American country with two capitals?

The only South American country with two capitals is Bolivia. Capital number one is its historic judicial capital, Sucre, and capital number two is Bolivia's administrative capital, La Paz.

What is the only true desert in Europe?

The Bledowska Desert in Poland is the only true desert in Europe. Located midway between Krakow and Czestochowa, it consists of 20 square miles of shifting sands and sparse vegetation.

Name the only Middle Eastern country without a desert.

Lebanon, renowned for its precious cedars, is the only Middle Eastern nation that has no desert.

Cite the only nation governed by "princes" and clerics.

Tiny Andorra, one of the world's oldest countries, is a principality nestled in the Pyrenees Mountains on the French-Spanish border. The nation is under the protection of both Spain and France, has been since 1278, and is governed by the bishop of Urgel, Spain, and the president of France (known in the past as "prince" of France) in what is called a co-principality. Andorra's flag reflects the blue and red of France is flag and the yellow and red of Spain's flag.

Where is the world's only jaguar preserve?

In 1996, the Cockscomb Basic Wildlife and Jaguar Preserve in Belize became the world's only jaguar preserve. The sanctuary is 150 square miles large and is home to about 200 of the endangered cats. Other wild residents at the Preserve include peccaries, howler monkeys, agouti, snakes, coatamundi, and over 300 species of bird.

Where is the world's only skin divers' shrine?

Some sixty feet down, at the watery bottom of Little Traverse Bay, in the small town of Petoskey, Michigan, is a life-sized figure of Christ. Located off U.S. Route 131, it is known as the Skin Divers' Shrine because it is so popular with the people who go skin diving in the bay. It is the only shrine of its kind.

Where can you find the only statue and popular tourist attraction of a little boy relieving himself?

Brussels, the capital of Belgium, is the only city to feature such a statue as a major tourist attraction. A colorful city, famous for its dark, rich beers, Brussels has in the town square a famous statue that depicts a little boy urinating. Known as the Mennekin Pis, or Peeing Boy, the statue, standing on a pedestal, is only twenty-four inches high. A continuous stream of water flows from the statue to the basin below. The Mennekin Pis was created in 1619 and has a wardrobe of 250 outfits. While in other places it might be frowned upon as a site for foreigners to visit, local citizens revere their little boy, who simply fell in love with one of their beers and let nature take its course.

Where is the only memorial in the world that contains a particular part of Hitler's body?

After the Fuehrer shot himself in the head on April 30, 1945, his charred remains were retrieved by the Russians. Dental technicians restored Hitler's rotting teeth and goldsmiths dipped them into a gold solution. Today, what appears to be two handsome bridges of solid gold teeth are preserved in the Russian World War II Moscow Archives, the only memorial that holds a piece of Hitler.

Which nation has the only national anthem that begins with a question?

The only nation whose national anthem opens with a question is the United States, whose national anthem, "The Star-Spangled Banner," begins with the question, "O say can you see...?"

Name the only country whose national flag is a single color.

The only country whose national flag is a single color—green—is Libya. Green is that nation's official color and also reflects the people's staunch devotion to Islam. The plain green flag was adopted in 1977.

Name the only country to have a single letter adorning its flag. Name the letter?

The only nation that has a single letter adorning its flag is the African country Rwanda. The letter *R* adorns its three-color flag, the colors being the Pan-African colors of red, yellow, and green. The *R* stands for Rwanda.

Name the only country whose national flag consists of a pair of triangular pennants.

The only nation whose flag is neither square nor rectangular but consists of two triangular pennants that are positioned one above the other is Nepal, in southern Asia. The two pennants, actually flown as a single flag, are crimson red.

Cite the only totally square national flag of the various nations that make up the United Nations.

The Swiss flag (Switzerland) is the only totally square national flag among U.N. countries. The Swiss flag resembles a red gift box; its center depicts a white cross. The only other country with a totally square flag, not a member of the U.N., is Vatican City. Switzerland, a nation famous for its chocolates, clocks and watches, secret numbered bank accounts, and skiing, was admitted to the United Nations on September 9, 2002, its newest member.

Name the only nation where a map of the country is depicted on the national flag.

The only country to display a map of the nation on its flag is Cyprus.

What is the only country in the world that has another country clean its streets and pick up its garbage?

The only country in the world that has another country clean its streets and pick up its garbage is the Vatican (officially Vatican City or the Holy See), which became a separate country in 1929 with the Lateran Treaty. Each day except Sunday, the city of Rome sends a sanitation crew to clean the streets of Vatican City and to collect its refuse. Members of the cleaning detail are obligated to present identification to Swiss guards upon entering and exiting Vatican City.

Name the only nation ruled by a duke.

The only country ruled by a duke is Luxembourg, ruled by Grand Duke Jean since 1964, following the abdication of his mother, Grand Duchess Charlotte.

What is the only country with an emperor?

The only country with a monarch with the title of emperor is Japan. Its present emperor, Akihito, succeeded to the imperial throne upon the death of his father, Emperor Hirohito. The Japanese no longer consider their emperors to be divine. Political power lies with the prime minister.

What is the only mountain that bears the name of a single letter and a single number?

The only mountain that bears the name of a single letter and number is K2, the world's second highest mountain (after Mount Everest). The *K* stands for the Karakoram range, which is part of the Himalayas. The *2* stands for the fact that the mountain is the second highest. The mountain's unofficial name is Mount Godwin Austen, after a British surveyor who measured the mountain in 1861. K2 was named by a Colonel T. G. Montgomery in 1856.

Name the only country where robots pay union dues.

The only country where robots pay union dues is Japan, which in the mid-1980s replaced workers with robots in union member factories. With threats of strikes and plant shutdowns, companies quickly came to terms with the nation's unions. They agreed to pay monthly union dues for every robot worker that replaced a union member for the duration of what would have been the union member's work life. Each robot yields union dues for human workers.

Cite the only country in the world whose emergency telephone number consists entirely of zeros—three of them.

Australia is the only country in the world where the emergency telephone number consists of three zeros (000), comparable to 911 in the United States. No other country's emergency telephone number contains only three zeros.

Where is the only place in the world in which a rhinoceros was voted to a city council?

On October 4, 1959, the citizens of São Paulo, Brazil, by a vote of just over fifty thousand, chose a female rhinoceros for the municipal council; she remains the only rhinoceros so honored. The people of São Paulo were protesting corrupt government, food shortages, and skyrocketing prices for the barest necessities. The rhino was brought in each day to the Municipal Building to attend meetings.

Name the only U.S. citizens who pay no taxes— federal, state, or city.

The only U.S. citizens who pay no taxes are Native Americans, providing they reside on Indian reservations. When a Native American buys items at a grocery store, book store, or gas station that isn't on the reservation, he or she has to pay the same taxes as everyone else.

What is the only country in Europe with the death penalty on its books?

Vatican City or the Holy See is the only European nation that has the death penalty on its books—kept there primarily as a historical document. It is against Catholic teaching to enforce the death penalty, but in centuries past executions had taken place at the Vatican for such crimes as heresy. The modern Vatican not only does not sanction the death penalty but also is an outspoken critic of such countries as the United States, China, Iran, and Muslim countries that use violence to satisfy violence. On numerous occasions Vatican City has won mercy for criminals about to be executed, noting the death penalty to be a barbaric and outmoded way of meting out justice.

Name the only state with a dead animal depicted on its license plate.

Maine license plates depict a "red" lobster; live lobsters are brownish-green. When cooked, most often boiled, a lobster's pigment turns red. Someone wasn't thinking, but, then again, the state has no interest in promoting live lobster. Tourists often visit Maine for the explicit purpose of dining on its famous crustacean.

Name the only **state that is allowed to fly its state flag at the same height as the United States flag.**

Texas is the only state that has the honor of flying their flag at the same height as the United States flag. The law stems from the Battle of the Alamo, 1836, when a Texas standard bearer gave up his life maintaining a raised Texas flag.

Where is the only diamond mine in the United States? It is also the only diamond mine in the world that is open to the public.

The only diamond mine in the States is the Murfreesboro Diamond Mine in Arkansas, better known as Crater of Diamonds State Park. The public is free to search for raw diamonds in a thirty-five acre field. Over 70,000 diamonds have been found there, including the 40.23 carat "Uncle Sam," the 16.37 carat "Amarillo Starlight," and the 15.33 carat "Star of Arkansas." Since Crater became a park in 1972, over 3,500 carats have been carried home by visitors. Digging tools are available for rent. Free identification and certification of diamonds are provided by park interpreters.

What is the only U.S. state that grows bananas and coffee?

The only one of the fifty states that grows bananas is Hawaii. No other state (not even Florida) grows the tropical fruit. Hawaii is also the only state that grows coffee in its Kona district.

Name the only state with an official snack. Cite the snack.

As of June 7, 2001, Utah became the only state to adopt an official state snack—Jell-O. Salt Lake City had traditionally been number one per capita in Jell-O consumption in the nation. A 2002 Winter Olympics pin featuring a bowl of green gelatin was so popular that green Jell-O quickly sold out. Bill Cosby, the Jell-O spokesperson for over twenty-five years, had campaigned for the choice.

What is the only U.S. town named after an Islamic revolutionary ?

Elkader, Iowa, is the only town in the United States named after an Islamic revolutionary. Abd-el-Kader led Algeria's resistance against France in the mid-nineteenth century. The Iowa town's founders chose El-Kader as a namesake because he was in the news often.

Name the only U.S. town whose street signs are in Finnish and which has the only television broadcast entirely in the Finnish language.

The only place in the United States where all the street signs are in Finnish and which has a Finnish weekly television broadcast spoken entirely in the Finnish language, *Finland Calling*, is the town of Negaunee in Michigan's Upper Peninsula (UP). The winters in the UP are very cold, with climate conditions similar to those in Finland, which is why so many Finns live in the region. In fact, the state of Michigan has upwards of 125,000 Finns living within its borders.

What is the only U.S. state whose motto, "In God We Trust," is also found on American coins?

The only state that has the same motto as the one found on American coins is Florida, which adopted the phrase in 1868.

What is the only U.S. state named after a duke?

New York State, named after the duke of York (England) who would become King James II of England, is the only U.S. state named after a duke. It was given its present name in 1664 when the British conquered the Dutch. Until that time New York had been named New Netherland. It became a state upon ratification of the Constitution in 1788.

What is the only town to be named for a U.S. president while he held office?

Lincoln, Illinois, is the only town to be named for a U.S. President while he held office. It was named after Abraham Lincoln in 1853, while he was President (1861-1865). Formerly Lancaster, Lincoln, Ilinois is also the first city to be named after this beloved assassinated President.

Name the only U.S. city that is accessible only by boat or by plane.

The only U.S. city accessible only by boat or by plane is Juneau, Alaska. Juneau is Alaska's third largest city. Covering 3,108 square miles, it is the largest city in the U.S. in terms of area.

What is the only U.S. town that takes its name from the three states it borders?

The only U.S. town that takes its name from the three states it borders—Kentucky, Ohio, and West Virginia—is Kenova, West Virginia.

What is the only town in the U.S. with the word *beach* in its name that is not near a beach?

The only such place is Beach City, Ohio, which is nowhere near any beach or ocean. The town is named after Henry Beach, who founded the midwestern site in 1872. Mr. Beach was a valley railroad engineer.

Name the only state capitals that rhyme with one another.

Austin (Texas) rhymes with *Boston* (Massachusetts). No other U.S. capitals rhyme with one another.

Name the only U.S. state that doesn't share any letters with its own capital.

The only U.S. state that shares no letters in common with its own capital is South Dakota, whose capital is Pierre.

History

Name the only female Egyptian pharaoh.

Hatshepsut, who reigned from 1486 to 1458 B.C., was the only female Egyptian pharaoh (throne name Maat-ka-re). She was proclaimed successor to her father Thutmose I upon his death and ruled with her stepson Thutmose III. Hatshepsut was regarded as a good and wise ruler.

Who is the only member of the Ptolemaic family to have spoken Egyptian rather than Greek?

The only member of the Ptolemaic family and dynasty to have spoken Egyptian (they normally had translators) was the famous Egyptian queen Cleopatra VII (69 to 30 B.C.). Cleopatra was of Greek ancestry, but was fluent in several languages.

Who was the only Roman emperor to have his mother executed?

The Roman emperor Nero (Nero Claudius Caesar Drusus Germanicus, A.D. 54 to 68) was the only Roman emperor to have his mother executed. Agrippina, his mother, was the sister of the famous Roman emperor Caligula, whom she had conspired against. For that she had been banished from Rome. When her uncle Claudius became emperor following Caligula's assassination, Agrippina returned to Rome. Claudius had his own wife executed for adultery and treason. Agrippina had designs on Claudius and married him, even though he was her uncle. She fulfilled her grand scheme by convincing Claudius to adopt her son Nero and appoint him as his heir designate. She then proceeded to poison Claudius in A.D. 54, setting the stage for her son Nero to become the new emperor of Rome (and the world). Agrippina then became an impediment during her son's reign. In A.D. 59, Nero, unable to tolerate his mother any longer, had her executed, the only Roman emperor to commit such an act.

What was the only circumstance under which the women of ancient Rome were by law required to wear the "male garment" known as the toga?

The women of ancient Rome were by law obligated to shed the female garment known as the *stola* in favor of the male toga if they were prostitutes. All prostitutes were also required to register with the authorities.

Name the only queen to have sat on both the French and British thrones, having married monarchs of both of these nations.

Queen Eleanor of Aquitaine is the only queen in history to have sat on both the French and British thrones. She married Louis VII of France (1137-1180), a marriage which was annulled in 1152. Eleanor then married Henry, duke of Normandy and count of Anjou, who would later become King Henry II of England (1154-1189). Henry introduced England to the Plantagenet Dynasty (1154-1399); the houses of Lancaster and York followed. Eleanor's marriage with Henry was to spawn some four hundred years of strife between England and France.

Who was the only British monarch to pawn his own crown to finance a war?

The only British monarch to pawn his own crown was Henry V, who in 1417 received eight hundred pounds from the Abbot of Westminster to finance the Hundred Years War, which had begun in 1337 and was fought between England and France. The crown was well undersold, having been encrusted with a number of costly jewels, but the troops, mostly knights, had to be paid, the armor had to be maintained, and horses and men had to be fed. The Hundred Years War is famous among other things for the Battle of Orléans and Joan of Arc. The French ultimately prevailed, driving England from their soil except at Calais.

Name the only six-fingered British royal figure.

The only six-fingered royal figure was Ann Boleyn (1501-1536), second wife of Henry VIII. Ann Boleyn always wore gloves in public to conceal the alleged sixth finger on her left hand. In 1536 Henry had Anne executed on trumped-up charges of adultery and treason. She had been wife number two of his six.

Name the only British monarch to reign but never to marry.

Elizabeth I (reigned 1558-1603) is the only British monarch to reign but never to marry. Indeed, there were a number of candidates for her hand in marriage who were not only handsome but of solid lineage. Elizabeth I was the daughter of Henry VIII and Anne Boleyn, who gave Henry a daughter on September 7, 1533. Elizabeth I was educated at the hands of Cambridge scholars and had the good sense to choose qualified advisers who guided the spinster queen's reign to solid success. Her name came to define the time in which she lived, the Elizabethan Age, an age of cultural progress and prosperity for England. On her deathbed she passed the crown to James VI of Scotland (who became James I of England), son of Mary Queen of Scots, whom she despised; it was a wordless confirmation, as the dying queen was unable to speak.

Who is the only person buried in Great Britain's Westminster Abbey in a vertical or standing position?

Dramatist Ben Jonson (1572-1637), by order of King Charles I, was granted his wish to be buried at Westminster Abbey. Due to either an alleged lack of space or Jonson's poverty at the end of his life, Jonson is buried standing up. The stone has a simple inscription, "O Rare Ben Johnson" (although his name is more commonly spelt Jonson).

What was the only New England state that was not invaded by the British during the Revolutionary War?

The only New England state not invaded by the British was New Hampshire.

Who were the only siblings to sign America's Declaration of Independence?

The only siblings to sign the Declaration of Independence (August 2, 1776) were the Lee brothers of Virginia, Francis and Richard Henry. Francis was a member of the Virginia House of Burgesses and served in the Continental Congress from 1775 through 1779. Richard was a senator from Virginia from 1789 to 1792. Both brothers were leaders in the American Revolution, and they shared the unique distinction of being the only siblings to have their signatures on America's most famous document. (Note: The Declaration of Independence bears fifty-six signatures, most of which were signed before July 2.)

Who is the only clergyman to have signed the Declaration of Independence?

The only clergyman to have signed the Declaration of Independence was John Witherspoon of New Jersey, an American Presbyterian minister. Witherspoon later became the president of the College of New Jersey, which is today known as Princeton University.

Name the only U.S. general to have been shot to death by his own men.

The only U.S. general to lose his life at the hands of his own men is Stonewall Jackson (Thomas Jonathan Jackson), a Confederate general. On the night of May 2, 1863, at Chancellorsville, Virginia, Confederate sentries, mistaking the general for an enemy soldier, shot Jackson while celebrating a victory over Union soldiers. Jackson lingered near death for four days, undergoing an operation that resulted in his arm being amputated. His limbs, badly impaired by gunshot wounds, were buried in Chancellorsville. The wounded general was being transported to Lexington, Virginia, when on May 6 he died and was buried on a hill at Lexington. Hence General Stonewall Jackson is buried in two different sites, Chancellorsville, Virginia, and Lexington, Virginia.

Who was "America's only Queen"?

Queen Ludia Liliuokalani of the Hawaiian Islands resgined from 1881-1893. She was deposed by the advocates of a Republic for Hawaii in 1893. The monarchy was replaced by the Republic of Hawaii in 1894 and annexed to the U. S. in 1898, where she lived as a deposed queen until her death in 1917.

Who are the only mother and daughter to have individually won Nobel Prizes?

The only mother and daughter to have won Nobel Prizes were the Curies, mother Marie and daughter Irène Joliot-Curie. Marie Curie won the Nobel Prize in physics with her husband, Pierre, and A. H. Becquerel in 1903 for their study of radiation; she won a second Nobel in 1911 in chemistry for the discovery of radium and polonium. Her daughter Irène won the Nobel Prize for Chemistry with her husband, Frédéric, in 1935 for the synthesis of new radioactive elements.

Name the only American to cost a king his British throne.

The only American to cost a British king his throne was American socialite Wallis Simpson of Blue Ridge Summit, Pennsylvania, whose romantic liaison with King Edward VIII of England in 1936 resulted in a constitutional crisis and the eventual abdication of the throne of England. The former king became the Duke of Windsor and Simpson became the Duchess of Windsor. They wed in 1937, settling in Paris, France. Edward VIII became forever estranged from the British royal family. (Note: Simpson was a divorcée, married twice before; the second time in 1928 to Ernest A. Simpson, hence her last name.)

What was the only historical event from which someone paid almost $30,000 for a piece of cake?

The only piece of cake to cost just under $30,000-in actual sale price $29,900—was a piece of the wedding cake, a memento from the royal wedding of Edward VIII and Wallis Simpson, the duke and duchess of Windsor (England), married June 3, 1937. The piece of wedding cake, preserved in its original box for sixty-seven years, was sold at Sotheby's Auction, and bid for on February 7, 1998, by Benjamin and Amanda Yin of the United States, with proceeds donated to charity.

What is the only group of World War II behind-the-scenes experts to receive the rare Congressional Gold Medal?

Navajo Indians known as Code Talkers in World War II—were the only group of experts to receive the Congressional Gold Medal. No code in the Navajo language was ever broken during the war. The Code Talkers were awarded their medals by George W. Bush in July 2002. (Note: The Congressional Gold Medal is solid gold!)

Name the only country against which Germany "officially" declared war during World War II.

On December 11, 1941, four days after the United States lost most of its Pacific naval fleet at Pearl Harbor, Germany declared war on the United States. Hitler believed the bombing of the U.S. fleet at Pearl Harbor had so weakened the United States that it would be too sidelined to mount a decent offensive. The United States is the only country on which Germany "officially" declared war.

Name the only Middle Eastern country to sign a friendship pact with Nazi Germany during World War II.

Turkey, on June 18, 1941, is the only Middle Eastern country to sign such a pact with Nazi Germany. In 1945, Turkey switched sides and belatedly gave its allegencies to the Allies.

What is the only Axis nation the United States did not declare war on?

During World War II the only Axis nation that the United States did not declare war on was Finland.

Name the only royal figure whose airspace above his country was deemed sacred.

During World War II Emperor Hirohito of Japan had deemed his airspace sacred and inviolable. Even though the portion of the atmosphere over the emperor's palace was what might be referred to as a "no fly zone," the famed Lieutenant Commander James "Jimmy" Doolittle of the U.S. Army Air Corps violated it. On April 18, 1942, Doolittle conducted air raids on Tokyo and other Japanese cities, thus trespassing on the sacred airspace. Japan retaliated by slaughtering as many as 250,000 Chinese peasants whom Japan believed were sheltering the U.S. pilots after the raid.

Name the only U.S. married couple to have been executed for treason.

The only married couple sentenced to death in the United States for treason, the stealing of atomic bomb secrets for the Soviet Union, was the Rosenbergs, Ethel and Julius. They were executed on June 19, 1953, at Sing Sing Prison in Ossining, New York. Ethel was the last women in the northeast United States to have been executed on the electric chair. Rosenbergs left behind two sons, Robert and Micheal.

Who is the only foreign statesman to have been made an honorary citizen of the United States?

In 1963 Sir Winston Churchill, former Prime Minister of Great Britain, became the only foreign statesman to have been made an honorary citizen of the United States. President John F. Kennedy awarded him the honor.

Who are the only two women who have shared a Nobel Prize?

The only two women to share the Nobel Prize were Mairead Corrigan and Betty Williams of Ireland, who in 1976 won the Nobel Prize for Peace for their tireless efforts to bring peace and harmony to Northern Ireland.

Who is the only American commoner to become queen of an Islamic nation?

Lisa Halaby, on a visit to the Islamic country of Jordan in the Mideast, landed the nation's throne. She and the recently widowed King Hussein fell in love. The former Princeton graduate—at twenty-six— wed the King. On June 15, 1978, the former Christian converted to Islam. Lisa Halaby was renamed "Queen Noor"—*noor* means "light" in Arabic. It is the only time an American commoner became queen of an Islamic nation.

Where was the only brain-dead prince named king of a nation? Who was he?

On June 9, 2001, Royal Crown Prince Dipendra of Nepal, in a fit of rage after a family quarrel over the bride his family had chosen for him, shot dead most of the members of his royal family. Among the victims were King Birenda, his father, and Queen Aiswarya his mother. He then turned an automatic weapon on himself. Although he was brain dead, the Nepalese Privy Council named Crown Prince Dipendra king of Nepal in an emergency conclave. The gesture may have been nothing more than symbolic, for Crown Prince Dipendra was beloved by the people of Nepal, who felt that he cared for the poor of the country and was known to have mixed with commoners. Crown Prince Dipendra died the following day, the only brain-dead prince to be made king.

Literature, Theater & Dance

Who is the only person to have won both a Nobel Prize and an Oscar?

Irish-born writer George Bernard Shaw (1856-1950) is the only person to have won both prizes. He won the Nobel Prize in literature in 1925 for what the Nobel committee called "his work which is marked by both idealism and humanity, its stimulating satire often being informed with a singular poetic beauty." Shaw was awarded the Oscar for best screenplay in 1938 for *Pygmalion*, the film version of his play of the same name. Wendy Hiller played Eliza Doolittle, the lower-class girl Professor Higgins bet he can teach to speak proper English and thus pass off as a lady. The story formed the basis of the later musical and film *My Fair Lady*. Other works by Shaw include *Saint Joan, Major Barbara*, and *Man and Superman*.

Name the only modern author once imprisoned by cannibals.

Herman Melville (1819-1891), author of *Moby- Dick* (1851), is the only modern author to have been imprisoned by cannibals. In 1839 he went to sea as a cabin boy. Ill-treated, he deserted ship (1841-1842), taking refuge on the Marquesas Islands, where he was befriended by cannibals. Unhappy, Melville wished to leave the islands, but his hosts objected, imprisoning him. On August 9, 1842, Melville escaped from Typee Valley, knowing full well he was to be eaten if he remained there. His story *Typee* (1846) depicts quite vividly his adventures among the cannibals. Thus, Herman Melville, the only author to be imprisoned by cannibals, would not have been able to write the famous tale of the great white whale had he not found freedom from his captors.

Name the only author to publish at least one book in every category of the Dewey decimal system.

Isaac Asimov (1920-1992) is the only author to have a book in every single Dewey decimal system category. Asimov wrote over five hundred books in his lifetime, including the famous Foundation series and *The Gods Themselves*.

Who was the only writer to voluntarily turn down a Nobel Prize in literature?

Jean-Paul Sartre of France (1905-1980) was offered a Nobel Prize in literature in 1964. He was the only honoree to turn down the prize voluntarily, on the grounds that such honors could interfere with a writer's responsibilities to his or her readers.

Who is the only novelist to have received three National Book Awards?

Saul Bellow is the only novelist to have received three National Book Awards, for *The Adventures of Augie March* (1954), *Herzog* (1965), and *Mr. Sammler's Planet* (1971). In 1975, he also won the Pulitzer Prize for his novel *Humboldt's Gift*. The Nobel Prize in Literature was awarded to him in 1976. The prestigious National Book Award is awarded annually by the National Book Foundation for the best work of fiction in the United States.

Which American Indian tribe has given the world the only known Indian alphabet? Which individual of this unique tribe is credited with inventing this alphabet?

The Cherokee Indians, who lived in the southeastern United States, gave the world the only known Indian alphabet. The inventor of the Cherokee alphabet was Cherokee scholar George Guess, better known by his tribal name Sequoya, who formulated the eighty-five-character syllabary in 1821. Sequoya (sometimes spelled Sequoyah) was also honored by Hungarian botanist Stephen Endlicher (1804-1849), who classified giant redwood trees of California as genus Sequoia after the Cherokee scholar, thus also making Guess the only American Indian to have a type of tree named after him. (Note: The only state where the giant redwood Sequoia trees are found is California.)

Who is the only American playwright to have won the Nobel Prize for literature?

Eugene Gladstone O'Neil (1888-1953) was the only American playwright to have won the Nobel Prize for literature (1936). *The Iceman Cometh* and *Long Day's Journey Into Night* are among his famous plays that deal deeply with the complexity of the human psychology. O'Neill also won the Pulitzer Prize for drama three times.

Name the only book written by a teenager that was made into a Broadway play and that went on to win a Pulitzer Prize and a Tony Award for best play.

The Diary of Anne Frank, originally titled *The Diary of a Young Girl*, was written by sixteen-year-old Anne Frank, who died on March 16, 1945, at Bergen-Belsen, a German concentration camp. Her book *The Diary of a Young Girl* was published in Holland in 1947. In October 1955, the play *The Diary of Anne Frank* opened on Broadway at the Cort Theatre with actress Susan Strasberg portraying Anne Frank. The play won both a Pulitzer Prize (1957) and a Tony Award for best play.

Name the only theater in the world to contribute military props to its nation's defense.

The only theater anywhere to contribute military arms to a nation's defense in wartime was the Drury Lane Theatre in London, England. In 1940 the British were short of men and weapons. Through the Home Guard they enlisted over a million volunteers. The government raided such unlikely sources as military museums and war memorials, acquiring such antiquated hardware as swords and revolvers—Colt .45s used one hundred years before in the old American West. The Drury Lane Theatre got in touch with the Home Guard to make the minute contribution of twelve rusty rifles, which were stage props. The government would find use for the rifles and promised to return them after the war.

What is the only Shakespeare play that was made into a science fiction film? Name the film.

The only Shakespeare play made into a science fiction film is *The Tempest* (1611). The film is *Forbidden Planet* (1956), which stars Walter Pidgeon, Anne Francis, Earl Holliman, and Jack Kelly. It's about an expatriate (Pidgeon) with a daughter (Francis) and a robot—Robby the Robot. They build an empire and are visited by space travelers. While liberties are taken concerning the bard's opus, the film has become a minor classic, singled out for its special effects and eerie electronic music.

Who is the only writer to have won an Oscar, Tony, and Edgar?

Sidney Sheldon is the only writer to have won an Oscar, Tony, and Edgar. He has sold more than 300 million books, including bestsellers *Best Laid Plans* and The *Other Side of Midnight*. He also has had a listing in the Guinness Book of World Records as the world's most-translated writer (51 languages).

When was the only time a husband and wife were shortlisted at the same time for the famed Whitbread Book of the Year literary prize?

The only time a husband and wife were shortlisted together for the Whitbread literary prize was in 2003. Claire Tomalin, author of *Samuel Pepys:The Unequalled Self*, a biography of the diarist Pepys, competed against her husband Michael Frayn, who wrote *Spies*, a World War II novel. Tomalin won. The Whitbread prize is open to authors from the UK and Ireland and divided into five categories: novel, first novel, biography, poetry and children's book.

Can you name the only African-American to have won two Pulitzer Prizes?

Playwright August Wilson is the only African-American to win two Pulitzer Prizes. In 1987 he won the Pulitzer Prize for drama for his play *Fences*, which was produced on Broadway at the 46th Street Theatre. The play also won a New York Drama Critics Circle Award. In 1990 Wilson again won the Pulitzer Prize for drama for his play *The Piano Lesson*, produced on Broadway at the Walter Kerr Theatre. He was born in Pittsburgh in 1945 to a white father and a black mother. He flunked out of ninth grade yet went on to win two Pulitzer Prizes, the only African American so honored.

Can you name the only **father and daughter to each have shows on Broadway at the same time in which each wrote the music?**

The only father and daughter to each have a show on Broadway at the same time, for which each one wrote the music, were Richard Rodgers and his daughter, Mary Rodgers. She wrote the music to *Once Upon a Mattress*, starring Carol Búrnett and playing at the Alvin and Winter Garden Theatres in 1960, after having moved up from an off-Broadway house. Her father, Richard Rodgers, wrote the music to *The Sound of Music* on Broadway from 1959 to 1965 at the Lunt Fontaine Theatre.

Name the only composer and lyricist to be made honorary members of an American Indian tribe for their work on a Broadway show.

On November 25, 1946, in a ceremony presided over by Oklahoma governor Robert S. Kerr, composer Richard Rodgers and lyricist Oscar Hammerstein were made honorary members of the Kiowa Indian tribe. The Kiowa Indians were honoring them for their creation of the musical *Oklahoma!* From that point onward, Rodgers and Hammerstein and their families were allowed to visit the Kiowa reservation year round and enjoy Kiowan hospitality.

Can you name the only ballet dancer to garner the title "Prima Ballerina Assoluta"?

Dame Margot Fonteyn (1919-1991) of Great Britain was accorded the august title of Prima Ballerina Assoluta by the Royal Ballet. She was born in Reigate, Surrey, England, as Margaret Hookham. In 1934 after studying in London with a Russian teacher and dancer, she became a member of Victor Wells Ballet, later known as Sadler's Wells Ballet, and finally, as the Royal Ballet. By 1940 she had become prima ballerina, first or principal dancer, and in 1979 earned the title *prima ballerina assoluta*, meaning absolutely the first or top ranking dancer in the history of the art. Never before or since has a dancer been so honored.

Can you name
the only premier danseur to
be born on a train?

The only premier danseur to be born on a train is Rudolf Nureyev (1938-1993), whose mother gave birth to him while the train was speeding through the Ural Mountains, located in western Russia. He was the first dancer during the Cold War period to defect to the West.

The Military

Name the only nation in the world in which women, by law, must submit to the military draft.

In Israel, since the birth of the nation on May 14, 1948, women have been required to submit to the draft. The exceptions are the same as for their male counterparts, with motherhood also exempting females. Women are not assigned to combat duty, although carrying and using firearms is mandatory for both genders.

Name the only nation without an army or military yet where able-bodied males are conscripted soldiers.

Switzerland is the only country without an army or military, yet where every able-bodied male from age twenty to sixty is automatically a soldier.

What is the only country whose entire military consists of foreign-born soldiers?

The Vatican, whose military consists of Swiss guards, all Swiss born, is the only country whose military consists of foreign-born soldiers. They have been guardians of the Holy See since 1506 under Pope Julius II ("The Warrior Pope"). It was actually Pope Sixtus IV who in 1478 enlisted the Swiss military to protect the Vatican and its treasures. This arrangement is sanctioned by Switzerland, has held for centuries, and is the only one of its kind.

Name the only nation whose constitution forbids maintaining an army.

The only nation whose constitution forbids maintaining a national army is the Central American country Costa Rica. This small nation, a leader in its public health system and high literacy rate, by law cannot raise an army. Their belief is that an army promotes the formation of a police state, causing the suspension of civil rights. The army was abolished in 1949, leaving Costa Rica with only a civil guard and a rural guard.

Cite the only commissioned female in the Confederate army.

Sally Louisa Tompkins (1833-1916) was the only woman to hold a commission in the Confederate army. Because of her tireless work to maintain a hospital she herself opened Confederate President Jefferson Davis had her commissioned as a captain in the Confederate service on September 9, 1861, thus earning her the name "Captain Sally." Upon her death, she was buried with full military honors.

Name the only U.S. general to bring his wife and pets into a military camp in the midst of a war.

General George Armstrong Custer (1839-1879), feeling lonely, defied military rules by bringing his wife Elizabeth Bacon Custer (Libby) and their pets (dogs, goats, squirrels and a raccoon) to military camp. Libby allegedly insisted that she not be left behind and even joined her husband in the field when it was safe to do so. Custer died fighting the Native Americans at the Battle of Little Bighorn in 1879.

Name the only Green Beret to top the *Billboard* chart.

Staff Sergeant Barry Sadler was serving in the U.S. Army Special Forces as a Green Beret when in 1966 he completed "The Ballad of the Green Berets," which shot to the number one position on Billboard's Hot 100 on March 5, 1966, staying there just over a month until it yielded the prestigious slot to The Righteous Brothers. "The Ballad of the Green Berets" inspired homesick Vietnam GIs and literally put the Green Berets Special Forces on the military map. It was vitally instrumental in making John Wayne's motion picture *The Green Berets* a number one box office smash hit. On September 7, 1988, while serving in Guatemala, Sadler was seriously wounded—a gunshot to the head as he climbed into a taxi. He lingered near death for more than a year before he passed away. "The Ballad of the Green Berets" has not only become a modern music classic, but has helped make the Green Berets a revered unit of the U.S. Army.

Where is the only place during World War II where the U.S. Marines' official uniform included a kilt?

Samoa in the South Pacific is the only place where the U.S. Marines' uniform included kilts, which, because of the torrid climate, were more comfortable than the usual pants. The kilts were actually akin to Samoans' native dress.

What is the only U.S. state that did not have a battleship named after it in World War II?

Montana is the only state that did not have a battleship named after it in World War II. All other states during that time were represented by a battleship. (Note: Hawaii and Alaska were not states at the time.)

During World War II American servicemen stationed in what country were the only U.S. GIs to be issued skis?

American GIs stationed in Iceland were the only U.S. servicemen to be issued skis.

Identify the only first lady to write a wartime film script or screenplay.

Eleanor Roosevelt wrote *Women in Defense* (1941), designed to convince women to enlist in the armed forces during World War II. The film was narrated by Katharine Hepburn and shown in movie houses with the regularly billed films. *Women in Defense* resulted in an increase in women enlisting in the military for the U.S. war effort.

Name the only Medal of Honor winner to receive top star billing in a film about World War II in which he played himself.

Audie Murphy, the most decorated U.S. war hero in any war, is the only Medal of Honor winner to star in a film in which he plays himself. The film *To Hell and Back* (1955) was based on his runaway bestseller book of the same name. It dramatizes Murphy's World War II exploits. Murphy's performance was one of the greatest film debuts by a nonactor, marking the beginning of a successful film career. A British film critic compared Murphy with both James Dean and Marlon Brando. The war hero and actor lost his life in a plane crash in 1970 and is buried in Arlington National Cemetery outside Washington, D.C.

Name the only British general buried at Arlington National Cemetery and the only U.S. soldier buried at St. Paul's Cathedral in London.

The only British general buried at Arlington National Cemetery is Major General Orde Wingate, who lost his life in a plane crash on March 24, 1944, in Burma. The only American soldier buried at St. Paul's Cathedral in London, England, is RAF pilot William M. Fiske III, shot down on August 16, 1940, in the Battle of Britain. Fiske was the first American to join the Royal Air Force.

Who was the only American to have won the Medal of Honor, Distinguished Service Cross, Distinguished Service Medal, and the National Security Medal?

The only American to win the Congressional Medal of Honor, the Distinguished Service Cross, the Distinguished Service Medal, and the coveted National Security Medal was William Donovan. Known as "Wild Bill," Donovan was the man who organized the famous OSS or Office of Strategic Services (1942-1945), which would become the U.S. Central Intelligence Agency, better known as the CIA. Donovan was a U.S. Army general. It is the National Security Medal for his work with the OSS that made him a unique American. "Wild Bill" Donovan passed away in 1959, a much-admired figure in American history. The nickname reflects many of his actions, carried out without regard for his safety if it meant saving others. The 1979 television miniseries *A Man Called Intrepid* is about "Wild Bill" Donovan.

Name the only U.S. general to win a Nobel Peace Prize.

In 1953 General George C. Marshall won the prestigious Nobel Prize for what came to be known as the Marshall Plan, the rebuilding of ravaged Europe after World War II.

When and where was the only nuclear bomb dropped by accident in the continental United States?

On May 22, 1957, a U.S. Air Force B-36, due to an improperly placed safety device, unloaded a Mark 17 nuclear bomb, over a (fortunately) uninhabited area in a desert region just outside of New Mexico. The bomb created a huge crater on impact, but failed to detonate as precautions were in place against such accidents. The nuclear bomb was being transferred to a secret location when the mishap occurred. The public only learned of the accident years later under the Freedom of Information Act. It only happened once that a nuclear bomb was dropped by accident on a nonmilitary, unrestricted area on U.S. soil.

When was the only time that an American U-2 spy plane was shot down by a foreign power.

The only time a U-2 spy plane was ever shot down by a foreign power was on May 1, 1960, when the U-2 American spy plane piloted by Francis Gary Powers was brought down by Soviet military gunfire. Powers managed to bail out but was taken prisoner. Premier Nikita Khrushchev was so enraged about the prospect of American espionage that he called off the much-touted Paris summit conference scheduled to take place between the United States and the Soviet Union. The incident was an embarrassment to the Eisenhower administration. Powers was eventually released, but the incident only fueled the Cold War, a deep-seated mistrust between the United States and the Soviet Union.

Name the only nun to have once been a U.S. Marine drill instructor and the most decorated woman of the Gulf War.

The former Mary Perrot, a U.S. Marine drill instructor and gunnery sergeant who served with the Marines during the Gulf War (1991-1992), is the only nun to have once been a U.S. Marine and the most decorated woman of the Gulf War. She was the recipient of the Gulf War Sea Service Ribbon, the Bronze Star Unit Ribbon, liberation military ribbons from the nations of Kuwait and Saudi Arabia, the Southeast Asia Ribbon with Three Stars, the Navy Achievement Ribbon with a Gold Star, and both the Marine and Navy Unit Commendation Ribbons. Perrot, at age forty-five, retired from the armed forces in 1999 after twenty years of distinguished service. She entered the Convent of the Order of the Ursuline Sisters in Louisville, Kentucky, as Sister Mary Perrot with the purpose of *helping* God by *serving* the poor.

Cite the location of the only overseas U.S. air base not situated in a country.

Diego Garcia, an island located in the Indian Ocean, where the United States maintains one of its most vital air bases, is the location of the only U.S. air base not found in a country.

Movies
& the
Academy
Awards

Where is the only movie house that shows only silent films?

The only movie house anywhere that shows only silent films is the Silent Movie Theatre, as it is appropriately named, located in downtown Los Angeles. On any given day, this theater shows such films as D. W. Griffith's *Intolerance* and *Birth of a Nation*, the films of Charles Chaplin such as *The Great Dictator*, Tom Mix films, and the films of Rudolph Valentino. One can see such silent film stars as Clara Bow, the "It Girl," and Mary Pickford, "America's Sweetheart" (though born in Canada). An organist and pianist are employed to accompany each film with music, just as it was in the 1920s.

Name the only official mint to create a coin that depicted an American film star in the nude.

Monnaie de Paris (Paris, France) is the only official mint to create a coin that depicted the American actress Marilyn Monroe in the nude. A memorial coin intended to honor the actress, it turned out instead to be an embarrassment to the French, as the actress's fans thought it was in bad taste. The coin, issued in 1990, was immediately withdrawn.

Name the only book that was written by a U.S. general and made into a film twice. Can you name the general?

Ben-Hur (1880) was written by Civil War Union Army general Lew Wallace. It was made into a film twice. In 1926 *Ben-Hur* was made into a silent film at a cost of $3.5 million, at the time the most expensive film ever made, starring Ramon Novarro as Judah Ben-Hur and Francis X. Bushman as Messala. A second version of *Ben-Hur* (1959) was made at a cost of $15 million, starring Charlton Heston as Ben-Hur, and Stephen Boyd as Messala. The film won the Oscar for best picture and a total of eleven Academy Awards, losing only the Oscar for best screenplay, which went to *Room at the Top*. Lew Wallace, the Civil War general and author, remains the only general in any military to have written a book twice filmed.

Name the only film in which Tarzan was forced to actually kill a crazed lion that was about to attack his costar.

On January 19, 1919, in the silent film *Tarzan of the Apes* starring Elmo Lincoln as Tarzan, an enraged lion was about to attack his costar Kathleen Kirkham when Lincoln stabbed the lion to death. Apparently, the drug given the animal had begun to wear off. It remains the only time a film Tarzan was forced to live up to his character's exploits, thus saving the life of the film's heroine.

What is the only silent film directed by Charles Chaplin in which he did not appear?

Chaplin always appeared in the films he directed, the lone exception being *A Woman of Paris* (1923). Nevertheless, this silent black and white film is considered a classic. The story concerns a woman who believes she has been jilted by her fiancé. The film features Edna Purviance, Adolphe Menjou, Clarence Geldart, and Carl Miller.

Name the only four-letter word spoken in a film that cost its producer $5,000 for the privilege of having it said on the screen. Cite the film, the actor who spoke the word, and to whom the word was spoken.

The only word that cost its producer $5,000 so that it could be said on screen was the word "damn," spoken by actor Clark Gable (as Rhett Butler) to Vivien Leigh (as Scarlett O'Hara) in the film *Gone with the Wind* (1939). In the very last scene of the four hour and thirty-minute film, Rhett, fed up with Scarlett's selfishness, has the last word before taking his permanent leave. When Scarlett asks where she will go, Rhett fires back, "Frankly, my dear, I don't give a damn." The last word, "damn," was met with opposition by the censorship office, the Motion Picture Producers and Distributors of America, headed by censor Will H. Hays. In a meeting with the producer of *Gone with the Wind*, David O. Selznick, Hays demanded a fine of $5,000 for a violation of the profanity code. Selznick paid the money rather than have Rhett Butler say, "Frankly, my dear, I don't care." This remains the only instance in film history in which $5,000 was paid for the use of one word, about $62,000 in today's currency.

Who is the only film actress with a major role in a major film to be barred from the film's premiere because of the color of her skin?

On December 16, 1939, Hattie McDaniel became the only actress to be forbidden to attend the premiere of a major film, *Gone with the Wind*, in which she was featured, and for which she subsequently won an Oscar for best supporting actress. The reason for her exclusion that McDaniel was African American. The premiere took place in Atlanta, Georgia.

Name the only person to have swum with the cartoon characters Tom and Jerry.

The only person to swim with Tom and Jerry on film was swimming star Esther Williams, the aquatic beauty. She swam with cartoon characters Tom and Jerry in the film *Dangerous When Wet* (1935) while performing an underwater sequence. That sequence turned out to be the best part of the film, drawing plaudits from critics for its imagination coupled with swimming sensation Williams who performed with panache alongside two of the most cherished animated creations in Hollywood.

Name the only film in which seven directors directed.

The only movie directed by seven people is *Forever and a Day* (1943), about a London house and the strange adventures of its occupants in pre-Dickensian London. The seven directors were René Clair, Edmund Goulding, Frank Lloyd, Victor Saville, Robert Stevenson, Cedric Hardwicke, and Herbert Wilcox. The film appears as one unit, not seven parts. It is a fast-paced film in which all the artists from actors to studio heads donated their services to the British War Relief Fund.

What is the only film for which a candy bar was named?

Love Me Tender (1956), starring Elvis Presley and Richard Egan, is the only film for which a candy bar was named. The candy bar "Love Me Tender" was made of milk chocolate and peanuts. It faded from store shelves within a few years after the film's debut. The wrapper, now worth over $100, featured a picture of the *Love Me Tender* cast.

What is John Wayne's only foreign film?

Brannigan (1975), directed by Douglas Hickox, is John Wayne's only foreign film. *Brannigan* is about an American policeman, played by Wayne, trying to apprehend an American criminal and take him back to the States. The film took place in London, England. Critics favored the film with good reviews. *Brannigan* is John Wayne's only foreign film in a career of over 150 films.

Name the only Oscar winner and knighted figure to have portrayed Adolf Hitler on the screen.

Sir Alec Guinness is the only Oscar winner and knighted figure to have portrayed Hitler on screen. He did so in 1973 in the film *Hitler, The Last Ten Days*. Having won an Oscar in 1957 for best actor in *The Bridge on the River Kwai*, Guinness was knighted by Queen Elizabeth II in 1959. Born in London in 1914, Sir Alec was lauded for his versatility as an actor and respected as a true gentleman. He won critical acclaim for, among other roles, the eight different parts he played in *Kind Hearts and Coronets* (1949). One of his most famous roles was that of Obi-Wan Kenobi in *Star Wars* (1977). Guinness died at the age of eighty-six in 2000.

Name the only film critic to have his review of a film written into the *Congressional Record*.

The film critic was Rex Reed, who at the time was writing movie reviews for the *New York Daily News*. The film was the Academy Award-winning documentary *Hearts and Minds* (1974), about the war in Vietnam. Reed had written a most poignant and eloquent literary discourse. So moving were Reed's words that the U.S. Congress bestowed upon him the unique distinction of entering his review into the *Congressional Record* for posterity.

Cite the only film premiere to be ushered by movie stars, such as Marilyn Monroe, Marlene Dietrich, Eva Marie Saint, and Celeste Holm.

A benefit for the Actors Studio at Broadway's Astor Theatre on March 9, 1955 marked the only time the ushers—all volunteers—consisted of celebrities such as Marilyn Monroe, Marlene Dietrich, Eva Marie Saint, and Celeste Holm. The occasion was the official premiere of *East of Eden*, a Warner Brothers film directed by Elia Kazan based on the John Steinbeck novel. The top-billed star was Julie Harris and the newcomer was James Dean. The celebrity ushers had promised not to give autographs. All the film's cast, with the exception of James Dean, were in attendance. Said Dean to a friend, "Why should I go [to the film's premiere]? I know I was good, and having people tell me so would only embarrass me."

Name the only film to use a scenting system known as "Aroma-Rama".

The 1959 documentary *Behind the Great Wall*, about the Great Wall of China, is the only film to use "Aroma-Rama." The fragrance used was an "Asian" fragrance, which was piped in through the air conditioning system. It was said the fragrance was from the lotus blossom. The gimmick lasted for the one film.

Name the only film to use "Smell-O-Vision".

Scent of a Mystery (1960), which starred Peter Lorre, Denholm Elliott, and Beverly Bently, is the only film to use "Smell-O-Vision." Perfume and tobacco odors were piped into individual seats with the Smell-O-Vision being activated when the movie patron pulled in the seat to sit down. The odors of *Scent of a Mystery*, perfume and tobacco, figured prominently in the film's story, set in England, about the quest to save a potential murder victim. As the drama increased, the perfume and tobacco odors became more pronounced and served as clues. Smell-O-Vision lasted for only one film, *Scent of a Mystery*.

What is the only film to feature "Odorama"?

The film *Polyester* (1981), starring Divine, Tab Hunter, and Edith Massey, a bizarre cult film that pokes fun at institutions, is the only film to use "Odorama." The scent was used by one of the characters in the film who would "sniff" out the future, as it were. Audience members were given scratch and sniff cards and, according to specific numbers which were flashed on the screen, would scratch the cards and sniff. Odorama was gone in a whiff, having been employed only for *Polyester*, which now shows up at cult film festivals.

Name the only Hollywood star to have created a World War II weapon that was patented.

Screen actress Hedy Lamarr is the only Hollywood film star to have created a World War II weapon for which she was awarded a patent. She starred in *Samson and Delilah* with Victor Mature and *The Female Animal*, as well as other films. In 1940 Lamarr, who had learned weaponry from one of her husbands, Fritz Mandl, sought the assistance of film composer and friend George Antheil in creating the weapon. It was a jamming device, which used rolls of paper with perforations that duplicated the split-second hops of radio frequencies, vital in weapons that depended on guidance, such as radio-controlled torpedoes. Patent number 2,292,387 belongs to Lamarr and was vital during World War II in defeating the enemy at sea. Lamarr's invention was kept top secret until 1999. She remains the only Hollywood star to invent a military weapon.

What is the only film that was made in 3-D (three dimensions) by Alfred Hitchcock?

Dial M for Murder (1954), starring Ray Milland, Grace Kelly, John Williams, and Robert Cummings, was the only Hitchcock movie filmed in 3-D.

Name the only film starring Marilyn Monroe in which the character she portrayed was nameless.

The only movie starring Marilyn Monroe in which her character did not have a name was *The Seven-Year Itch* (1955). Throughout the entire film (her twenty-third) she was referred to as "the girl."

Cite the only known case of one film star breaking another's tooth with too powerful a screen kiss during a passionate love scene.

It happened to screen actress Lana Turner, who lost a tooth as a result of receiving too powerful a kiss from her costar Anthony Quinn in the 1960 film *Portrait in Black*. The story involved a doctor, played by Quinn, who falls in love with a high society woman, played by Turner. The liaison leads to adultery and murder. Lana Turner is the only star to lose a tooth from too passionate a kiss on screen.

Can you name the only actor/film star whose actual birth name was "Hollywood"?

Actor Lyle Talbot, born Lyle Hollywood Henderson in Pittsburgh, Pennsylvania, in 1902, is the only actor/film star actually named Hollywood. A leading man in mostly "B" films, he changed his name to Lyle Talbot when he came under contract to Warner Brothers. He appeared in many films as leading man and featured parts, including *The Jackpot* (1950), *Purple Heart Diary* (1951), *There's No Business Like Show Business* (1954), *The Great Man* (1957), and *Sunrise at Campobello* (1960). He also appeared on television in shows such as *The George Burns Show* and *Ozzie and Harriet*. Lyle Talbot remains the only actor whose real name was Hollywood.

Can you name the only actor to have his nose insured?

Actor/comedian Jimmy Durante (1893-1980) took out an insurance policy for $100,000 against an injury to his nose. Durante's oversized, bulbous nose was integral to his career; after all, his nickname was "Schnozzola." He is remembered for his trademark, signing off on television, "Goodnight, Mrs. Calabash, wherever you are."

What is the only Bond film in which James Bond married?

It was in *On Her Majesty's Secret Service* (1969) that James Bond married. The beautiful young lady Teresa Draco who was his bride was killed in the film; hence it was a short-lived marriage. No other woman in the Bond flicks was able to snare the romantic James Bond for good.

Name the only actress who at her death was laid to rest while it was drizzling, and mourners observed the scene under umbrellas—an identical situation to the send-off accorded her in one of her starring roles.

Actress Ava Gardner was buried on January 29, 1990, at Sunset Memorial Park, Smithfield, North Carolina. The mourners—some two hundred—endured drizzle as they bid the onetime superstar a final farewell. In the 1954 film *The Barefoot Contessa*, Gardner had played a beautiful Spanish dancer who dies and is buried amidst inclement drizzly conditions, the mourners in the scene standing about under umbrellas.

Cite the only spoken word in Mel Brooks's *Silent Movie*. Who spoke the word?

In Mel Brooks's zany flick *Silent Movie* (1979), French mime king Marcel Marceau shouted, "No!" It was ironic for two reasons: Marceau, like American funny man Harpo Marx, never speaks while in character, and the film is titled *Silent Movie*.

Name the only film directed by horror author Stephen King.

Maximum Overdrive (1986) is the only film directed by Stephen King. Ninety-seven minutes long, the film featured Pat Hingle and Emilio Estevez. In the story, based on "Trucks" from his *Night Shift* collection of tales, trucks come alive and terrorize eatery diners with the usual King horror and suspense.

Name the only person to have a number one music album and a number one film at the box office in the same week.

Actress/singer Jennifer Lopez is the only person to have a number one music album and a number one film at the box office in the same week. It happened during the week of January 26, 2001, when she starred in the number one box office hit film *The Wedding Planner* and also had a number one album, *JLo*, which endured in that spot for two weeks.

Name the only actor to have a military aircraft bear his name or nickname.

The only actor to have a U.S. military aircraft bear his (nick)name is John Wayne. The Stealth helicopter in the U.S. Army flying arsenal is officially called "The Duke." It is designed specifically for reconnaissance missions and honors an actor whose films, such as *The Green Berets* and *The Sands of Iwo Jima*, often portrayed the U.S. military in a patriotic light.

When was the only time the Oscars were thrown in the trash?

The only time the Oscars were thrown in the trash was in 2000. That year, fifty-five Oscars had disappeared en route to the Academy of Motion Picture Arts and Sciences. Nine days before they were to be awarded at the Oscar ceremony, a junk salvager rummaging in a garbage container found fifty of the statuettes. The authorities were notified and a truck driver was charged with grand theft in the incident some days later.

Who was the only Oscar winner to have been a professional boxer and heavyweight world contender?

The only world heavyweight boxing contender and Oscar winner was Victor McLaglen. He won an Oscar for best actor in 1935 for his part in the film *The Informer* and fought Jack Johnson for the world heavyweight title to a no decision after six rounds in Vancouver, British Columbia, Canada, on March 10, 1909.

Cite the only film in which a harmonica score was Oscar nominated for best music. Its composer also performed the soundtrack.

Genevieve (1953), a British film, is now considered to be one of the best foreign films ever made. The harmonica score was written by composer and virtuoso performer Larry Adler. Adler, accused of having ties to communism, had his name omitted from American prints of the film and although his score was Oscar-nominated, it did not win.

Cite the only actress to have had twelve best actress Oscar nominations.

The only actress in Academy Award history to have had the distinct honor of being nominated twelve times for the best actress Oscar is Katharine Hepburn.

Name the only actor to have a film nominated for best picture and to also receive a best actor nomination for the film, but to lose in both categories and yet receive an honorary Oscar.

In 1946, Laurence Olivier directed and starred in the film *Henry V*. Olivier was nominated for best actor and *Henry V* was nominated for best picture. Both lost. Toward the end of the ceremony, however, an honororary Oscar was awarded to Olivier. Olivier was shocked, to say the least.

Who is the only royal figure to have won an Academy Award?

Her Serene Highness Princess Grace of Monaco is the only royal figure to have won an Academy Award. As Grace Kelly, prior to her marriage to Monaco's Prince Rainier III, she won an Oscar for best actress for her role in *The Country Girl* (1954), directed by George Seaton.

Name the only film composer to collect three Oscars in a single Oscar evening.

Pianist and composer Marvin Hamlisch is the only composer to win three Oscars at one award ceremony in 1973. The first Oscar was awarded to him for his original dramatic score to the film *The Way We Were*, starring Robert Redford and Barbra Streisand. His second Oscar was awarded for the original music for the song "The Way We Were" (lyrics by Alan and Marilyn Bergman). The third Oscar was for the original score to the film *The Sting*, starring Paul Newman and Robert Redford.

Name the only city where two actors were born whose names were Oscar and who were both nominated for Oscars.

The only actors to enjoy such a unique distinction were Oscar Homolka and Oskar or Oscar Werner, both born in Vienna, Austria. Oscar Homolka was born on August 12, 1898, and was nominated for an Oscar for the role of Uncle Chris in *I Remember Mama* (1948) in the supporting actor category, but lost to Walter Huston, who won for *The Treasure of the Sierra Madre*. Oscar (Oskar) Werner was born on November 13, 1922; he was nominated for his role in *Ship of Fools* in the best actor category but lost to Lee Marvin, who won for *Cat Ballou* (1965). Vienna is the only city where two actors were born with Oscar as their first names, who were both nominated for Oscars.

Cite the only Oscar year in which the votes had not been completely counted prior to the ceremony.

The year 1931 was the only year in which the votes had not been completely counted prior to the Oscar ceremony. Initially, the best actor Oscar was given to Fredric March for *Dr. Jekyll and Mr. Hyde*. The Oscar rules at the time stated that duplicate Oscars were to be awarded if a contender came within three votes of a winner on the final ballot. For his performance in *The Champ*, Wallace Beery came within one vote of March. This was discovered during the awards ceremony, and an announcement was made that both March and Beery were to be declared best actor for the 1931 film year. A new system was subsequently put in place with the votes tallied days before the Academy Awards ceremony.

Who is the only comedy team to win Oscars for their performance in a film?

Laurel and Hardy are the only comedy team to win Oscars for their performance in a film, *Music Box*, in 1931.

Name the only film director to win four Oscars.

John Ford is the only film director to win four Oscars. They were all for best director, as follows: *The Informer* (1935), *The Grapes of Wrath* (1940), *How Green Was My Valley* (1941), and *The Quiet Man* (1952).

Name the only non-American married couple to have won Oscars.

British actress Vivien Leigh (born in Darjeeling, India), and British-born Lord Laurence Olivier are the only non-American actors in the history of Oscardom to be married to each other and to each have won an Oscar. Leigh won her Oscar in 1939 for her role as Scarlett O'Hara in *Gone with the Wind*. Olivier won his first Oscar for acting in *Hamlet* in 1948; the film also won for best picture. Leigh passed away in 1967. Olivier passed away in 1989. The couple had divorced in 1960.

Cite the only time in which the Academy Awards were published by a newspaper before the awards ceremony took place.

In 1939 (the *Gone with the Wind* year), the *Los Angeles Times* broke its word with the Academy and published the names of the winners two hours before the awards ceremony. Ever since that year, no one but the public accounting firm PricewaterhouseCoopers knows the names of the winners beforehand.

Name the only brothers to win Oscars for the same film. Name the category.

The Epstein brothers, Julius and Philip, who won Oscars for their 1942 screenplay *Casablanca*, are the only brothers to receive Oscars for the same film. Sometimes the brothers were reported to have been twins, but although they may have looked alike, Philip was born in 1912, while Julius was born in 1909. The Epsteins had a fruitful collaboration until the death of Philip in 1958.

What is the only film with a title in Latin to be nominated for the best picture Oscar?

The only film with a Latin title to be nominated for a best picture Oscar was the English language film *Quo Vadis?* (1951), which means "Where Are You Going?" or "Whither Goest Thou?" This was the question addressed to Jesus by Saint Peter in a vision of Christ, "*Domine quo vadis?*" ("Lord, whither goest Thou?"). The film starred Robert Taylor and depicted the life of the Emperor Nero, played by Peter Ustinov. *Quo Vadis?* is also the only Oscar-nominated film whose title asks a question.

Name the only actor to be nominated for the best actor Oscar four years in a row.

Marlon Brando is the only actor to be nominated for a best actor Oscar four years in a row: in 1951 for *A Streetcar Named Desire*, in 1952 for *Viva Zapata!*, in 1953 for his role as Mark Antony in *Julius Caesar*, and in 1954 for his role as the over-the-hill prizefighter Terry Malloy in *On the Waterfront*, for which he finally won.

Name the only feature film in which actor James Dean won top billing but was not nominated for an Oscar.

Rebel Without a Cause, a Warner Brothers movie made in 1955 and directed by Nicholas Ray, is the only film for which James Dean had top star billing—his name, bold and large, was above the film's title—but he was not nominated for an Oscar. In his first major film, *East of Eden* (1955), actress Julie Harris was accorded top billing. Elia Kazan, who directed that film, found Dean to be rude and self-indulgent but perfect as Caleb "Cal" Trask in the film. Dean was nominated for best actor (posthumously).

Name the only film to win an Oscar for best screenplay in which not a word was spoken.

The only film ever to win an Oscar for best screenplay in which not a word was spoken was *The Red Balloon* (1955), with screenplay by Albert Lamoirissez. Though wordless, his tale concerns a lonely boy's love for a red balloon, which eventually lifts him heavenward. French-made and magically absorbing, the film has not lost its charm and charisma after almost fifty years. *The Red Balloon* has become a classic.

Name the only actor to have been a navy ensign in World War II and to win an Oscar portraying an ensign on the screen.

Jack Lemmon won an Oscar for best supporting actor playing Ensign Pulver in *Mr. Roberts* (1955), a comedy about oddball adventures on a naval vessel. It just so happens that Lemmon had been a commissioned officer with the rank of ensign during World War II, making him the only actor to have actually been an ensign as well as to have played that role in a film.

Name the only film with a biblical theme to win the best picture Oscar.

The 1959 film *Ben-Hur* won the Oscar for best picture and remains the only biblical film to accomplish this. *The Robe*, *The Ten Commandments*, *The Greatest Story Ever Told*, and John Huston's *The Bible* never won Hollywood's highest prize.

Who was the only star of two musicals in consecutive years, both of which were nominated for the best picture Oscar, and for both of which she was nominated for best actress?

The only actress to star in two musicals in consecutive years, both of which were nominated for the best picture Oscar, and for which she was nominated for the best actress Oscar, was Julie Andrews. In 1964 Andrews won the best actress Oscar for her role in *Mary Poppins*; the film lost the best picture Oscar to *My Fair Lady*. In 1965 Andrews was nominated for best actress for her role in *The Sound of Music*. The film won the best picture Oscar but the best actress Oscar went to another Julie, Julie Christie, for her starring role in *Darling*.

Cite the only time in Oscar history that the best picture came from the Broadway stage three years in a row. Give the years of the pictures.

My Fair Lady (1964), starring Rex Harrison and Audrey Hepburn, won the best picture Oscar. The play, starring Rex Harrison and Julie Andrews, had been a smash hit on Broadway. In 1965, *The Sound of Music*, starring Julie Andrews and Christopher Plummer, won the best picture Oscar. *The Sound of Music* had just come from the Broadway stage after a long run; its premiere stars were Mary Martin and Theodore Bikel. In 1966 *A Man for All Seasons* won the best picture Oscar; it starred Paul Scofield as Sir Thomas More. *A Man for All Seasons* had been on Broadway with Scofield in the leading part. This is the only period in Oscar history when in three consecutive years— 1964, 1965, and 1966—the best picture Oscars had originated on the Broadway stage.

Name the only dwarf to have been nominated both for an Academy Award and a Tony Award.

Actor Michael Dunn is the only dwarf to have been nominated for both awards. At just under three feet ten inches, Dunn was nominated for an Oscar in the supporting actor category for his film role as the compassionate observer in *Ship of Fools* (1965); he lost to Martin Balsam, who won for *A Thousand Clowns*. In the year before, Dunn had been nominated for a Tony Award for the part of a dwarf in the play *The Ballad of the Sad Café*; he lost to Hume Cronyn in *Hamlet*. As an actor Dunn fought to keep away from freak roles, courageously turning down parts that would exploit his height. Dunn appeared in numerous films and won the respect of his peers.

Name the only person to win an Academy Award for his work in an X-rated film.

Screenwriter Waldo Salt won Best Screenplay for the X-rated film *Midnight Cowboy* (1969), the only X-rated film to achieve the honor. *Midnight Cowboy* prevailed over strong competition, including *Butch Cassidy and the Sundance Kid*, *Hello Dolly*, and *Anne of a Thousand Days*. Actors in the film, Dustin Hoffman, John Voight, and actress Sylvia Miles were all nominated for Oscars, but didn't win. The Academy of Arts and Sciences no longer allows X-rated films or their cast members to qualify for an Academy Award.

Name the only Oscar winner to have been a Rhodes scholar.

Actor, songwriter, and singer Kris Kristofferson is the only Oscar winner to have been a Rhodes scholar. In 1954 Kristofferson went to Oxford University in England. In 1984 he won an Oscar for his original song score for the film *Songwriter*, in which he co-starred with Willie Nelson. The son of an army general, after a hitch in the army, the brainy Kristofferson embarked on a teaching career, teaching English at West Point Military Academy. He appeared in numerous films including *A Star Is Born* (1976) with Barbra Streisand.

Name the only motion picture based on the life of a music composer to win an Academy Award for best picture.

Amadeus (1984), based on the life of Wolfgang Amadeus Mozart, is the only motion picture based on the life of a composer to win an Oscar for best picture. *Amadeus* won seven Oscars including best screenplay, best director, and best actor for F. Murray Abraham.

Cite the only Oscar host to open the annual ceremony by insulting the audience. What did he say?

At the 1987 Academy Awards, Chevy Chase opened the ceremony by saying, "Good evening, Hollywood phonies." While the audience seemed to take the remark good-naturedly, one could sense the embarrassment that sent a chill through the auditorium. When Chevy makes public appearances, he is billed as Chevy Chase and not Cornelius Crane Chase, his real name.

Name the only person to have both won an Oscar and bought an Oscar.

Director Stephen Spielberg is the only person to have won an Oscar and to have bought one. On December 15, 1996, at Christie's auction house, he paid $550,000 for the Oscar won by Clark Gable for *It Happened One Night* (1934). The altruistic Spielberg then turned around and gave it as a gift to the Academy of Motion Picture Arts and Science, which bestows the Oscars. In a letter accompanying the gift, Mr. Spielberg wrote: "The Oscar is the most personal recognition of good work our industry can ever bestow, and it strikes me as a sad sign of our times that this icon could be confused with a commercial treasure." In 1993 Spielberg won an Oscar for best director for *Schindler's List*, which also won best picture and five other Oscars.

Who is the only actress to be nominated for both the best screenplay and the best actress Oscars in the same year?

In 1995 Emma Thompson was nominated for the best actress and best screenplay Oscars, both for the movie *Sense and Sensibility*. She won the Oscar that year for her screenplay, but lost the best actress Academy Award to Susan Sarandon, who was absolutely brilliant in *Dead Man Walking*.

Cite the only time two actors appeared in a film whose screenplay was written by them and for which they won an Oscar for best screenplay.

Ben Affleck and Matt Damon won an Oscar for best screenplay for *Good Will Hunting* (1997), the only time a pair of actors won an Oscar for the screenplay of a film in which they acted.

Who is the only fugitive from justice to win an Oscar?

On March 23, 2003, director Roman Polanski won the Oscar for Best Director for *The Pianist* (2002), a film about a concert pianist's experience in the concentration camps of Nazi Germany. Polanski himself survived the Holocaust as a child growing up in Poland. When Polanski's name was announced at the Academy Awards, a strange silence followed a loud ovation when the audience realized that Polanski was not present. Polanski has been a fugitive from U.S. justice since 1977 for statutory rape of a thirteen-year-old girl. He fled the country rather than go to prison and has not since returned. The Oscar was mailed to the director's home in France. Among Polanski's other famous films are *Rosemary's Baby* (1968), *The Exorcist* (1973), and *Chinatown* (1974).

Music

Name the only opera of the classical era to have been commissioned by a ruler of Egypt.

The only opera commissioned by a ruler of Egypt was the Giuseppe Verdi opera *Aida*. It was commissioned by Egypt's ruler, Khedive Ismail Pasha to mark the opening of the Suez Canal. The opera first opened in Cairo in 1871. After that it was performed at La Scala in Italy in 1872 and then at the Metropolitan Opera (the Met) in New York City in 1873.

Can you name the only musician with several different birthdays?

Louis Armstrong (?-1971) often said his birth date was July 4, 1900. When he applied for a Social Security card he gave his birth date as August 4, 1901. A copy of the newspaper the *Mississippi Rag* gave Armstrong's birthday as July 4, 1901. Armstrong's biographer Tad Jones searched baptismal records which indicate that Armstrong's true birthday is August 4, 1901.

Name the only opera whose subject matter is Eskimos.

Kaddara, composed in 1920 by Danish musician and composer Hakon Borrensen, is the only opera about Eskimos. Set in Greenland, *Kaddara* premiered in Copenhagen, Denmark, in the autumn of 1921.

What is the only nonelectric musical instrument invented in the twentieth century?

Invented in Trinidad in the 1930s, the steel drum is the latest nonelectric musical instrument and the only one invented in the twentieth century.

Who is the only opera singer to have two foods named after her?

The only opera singer to have two types of food named after her was Australian-born Dame Nellie Melba (1861-1931), one of the greatest sopranos of her time. She sang at La Scala in Italy and at the Metropolitan Opera House (the Met) in New York. The first food named in her honor is peach Melba, which consists of sliced peaches, ice cream, and heavy cream; the second is Melba toast, a thin, well-done toast.

Who is the only person to have received a Diamond Record Award from the *Guinness Book of World Records* for selling more records in more languages than any other artist in history?

In 1983 Julio Iglesias became the only performer ever to receive a Diamond Record Award from the *Guinness Book of World Records* for selling records in more languages than any other artist. The languages are Spanish, German, Japanese, English, Italian, Portuguese, French, and Tagalog.

Name the only state whose official song was written by one of its governors.

Louisiana is the only state whose official song was written by one of its governors. The song "You Are My Sunshine" was written by two-term governor Jimmie Davis (with Charles Michael) in 1940.

Name the only person to have been awarded a special Medal of Honor for writing songs.

George M. Cohan, by an Act of Congress in 1940, was awarded a special Medal of Honor for composing music and lyrics to the song "You're a Grand Old Flag." The song was written in 1906 for the Broadway musical *George Washington, Jr.*, and for *Over There* (1917), which honored the World War I American Expeditionary Force. Cohan is the only songwriter ever so honored.

Cite the only film for which a piano concerto was especially composed.

The only film for which a piano concerto was especially composed was *Hangover Square* (1945). The piano concerto written exclusively for the film was *Concerto Macabre*, composed by Bernard Herrmann. Cregar portrays a classical composer who loses his mind and murders women. The concerto is dark, dazzling, and bizarre. Fifteen years later Bernard Herrmann would write the eerie music to *Psycho*, the Alfred Hitchcock grand scare opus.

Who is the only musician for whom a kitchen appliance is named?

The only musician to have a kitchen appliance named after him is Fred Waring. The Waring blender bears his name, as he was its inventor in 1936. Fred Waring was also a world famous bandleader. He conducted his band, the Pennsylvanians, throughout the 1930s, '40s, and '50s. Waring and the Pennsylvanians still dot the nostalgia horizon of the Big Band Era. Many of their records can now be found on CDs, and the music of his kitchen blenders—Waring blenders—still sells well.

Who was the only music composer accidentally shot to death by an American soldier.

Anton Webern of the twelve-tone school of music, or what is sometimes referred to as the second Viennese school, is the only composer accidentally shot to death by an American soldier. In Mittersill, Germany, on the night of September 15, 1945, Webern was mistaken for his son-in-law, who was being investigated in a black market case, and was shot by an American soldier on sentry duty. What a tragic mistake, for Webern, along with Arnold Schoenberg and Alban Berg, was one of the vibrant creators of the avant-garde movement. Webern's *Concerto for Nine Instruments* and his *String Trio* ensure him a solid place in twentieth-century music history. It is ironic that the three close musical friends all met such cruel fates: Berg died of a bee sting, Schoenberg was bitter, broken-hearted, and struggled to survive, and Webern was shot dead in a case of mistaken identity, the only musical composer to suffer such a fate.

Name the only composer to write four songs with titles that also became motion picture titles.

The only composer to write four songs with titles that became motion picture titles was Irving Berlin. His song "Blue Skies" became the title song of the film *Blue Skies* with Bing Crosby in 1946. The song "White Christmas" became the title song of the film *White Christmas* in 1954, which also starred Bing Crosby. Berlin's song "Easter Parade" became the title song of the film *Easter Parade* in 1948 that starred Judy Garland. Finally, the song "There's No Business Like Show Business" inspired the film of the same title in 1954.

Who is the only celebrity to have been arrested on her deathbed?

Singer Billie Holiday was the only celebrity to be arrested as she lay dying at New York City's Metropolitan Hospital on July 5, 1959. The arrest was for "narcotic addiction," a crime back in the 1950s and 1960s. A policeman was placed outside the blues/jazz singer's hospital room. Holiday passed away on July 17, 1959. She was forty-four years old. Pure heroin was found hidden in a box of tissues beside her bed. Nicknamed "Lady Day," she had won instant fame with the song "Strange Fruit" (1939) and had appeared in the film, *New Orleans* (1947).

Name the only Christmas song written by Rodgers and Hammerstein.

The only Christmas song ever written by Rodgers and Hammerstein was "Happy Christmas Little Friend." The song was specifically commissioned by *Life* magazine's publisher as a gift to its readers. "Happy Christmas Little Friend" appeared in *Life* on December 29, 1952.

Name the only record album of Buddy Holly featuring Holly and released during the singer's lifetime.

The Chirping Crickets, released March 21, 1958 featured the group's number one single "That'll Be the Day" and its top ten hit "Oh Boy." Holly died in a plane crash on February 3, 1959.

Name the only father and daughter to each have a number one solo hit on Billboard's Hot 100 songs in the same year.

Frank Sinatra made it to number one on the *Billboard* charts with "Strangers in the Night," remaining number one from July 2, 1966, to July 15, 1966. In that same year "Ol' Blue Eyes'" daughter Nancy Sinatra had her own number one hit song with "These Boots Are Made for Walking." Nancy's song remained *Billboard's* number one song from February 26, 1966, to March 4, 1966, the only time a father and daughter each had a solo number one *Billboard* chart topper in the same year.

Name the only song by the Beatles named after a dog.

The Beatles tune "Martha My Dear" (1968) was named for an English sheepdog belonging to Paul McCartney.

Name the only Rhodes scholar to have penned the lyrics to a number one *Billboard* hit. Name the song, singer, and the most unusual circumstances concerning the singer.

Kris Kristofferson is the only Rhodes scholar (one who wins a special scholarship to England's Oxford University) to have penned the words to a number one *Billboard* hit, "Me and Bobby McGee," which was sung by his onetime love, Janis Joplin. Seeing its potential, Joplin included it among other songs on her album *Pearl*, which she was working on when she died of a drug overdose on October 4, 1970. The song stood out, and album producer Paul Rothchild had it cut into a single recording. "Me and Bobby McGee" made it to number one on the *Billboard* charts on March 20, 1971, a year after Joplin's death. It remained number one for two weeks, made more popular when the song's producer traded on the name of Kris Kristofferson. "Me and Bobby McGee" had been left behind by Kristofferson as a parting gift when he ended his relationship with Joplin. It is his only number one *Billboard* hit in any capacity, and he remains the only Rhodes scholar to chart a *Billboard* number one slot.

Name the only religious hymn played with bagpipes to surpass the million mark in copies sold.

"Amazing Grace," as performed on bagpipes by the Royal Scots Dragoon Guards in 1972, surpassed the million mark in albums sold. That the hymn or song was rendered via bagpipes made it unique; it is the only bagpipe version of a religious song to reach gold record status.

Who was the only member of the Beatles to have had his songs banned by the BBC?

The only member of the Beatles to have his songs banned by the BBC (British Broadcasting Corporation) was Paul McCartney. In fact, McCartney had two songs banned, both in 1972. Song one, "Give Ireland Back to the Irish," was deemed too political. The second single was called "Hi-Hi-Hi" and was considered too sexual.

What is Barbra Streisand's only *Billboard* chart topper that she sang with another women?

The only Streisand number one *Billboard* hit with another female was recorded with Donna Summer. The hit was "No More Tears (Enough Is Enough"), which topped the chart for two weeks, from November 24 until December 2, 1979. Press circles billed them as the "dueling divas," but the two singers conducted themselves graciously, as might be expected of two musical superstars and extraordinary singers.

Name the only American composer (and lyricist) to have lived past his one hundredth birthday.

Irving Berlin, born May 11, 1888, died at age 101 in 1989, the only American composer and Broadway lyricist to realize such a momentous milestone. His most famous songs were "White Christmas" and "God Bless America."

Radio &
Television

Name the only U.S. FM radio station with the identical letters of the city from which it broadcasts.

The only FM radio station that has the same letters as the city in which it broadcasts or where it is headquartered is WACO (Texas). When the radio station in Waco spells out its call letters, they just happen to form the name of the town from which it originates.

Name the only radio show to cause a panic among its listeners when it announced an invasion of Martians from space.

The star was Orson Welles, and the name of the show was *War of the Worlds* by H. G. Wells. The radio anthology program on which it appeared was *Orson Welles' Mercury Theater on the Air* and took place on CBS on Sunday evening, October 30, 1938. The Martians landed at the fictitious town of Grovers Mills, New Jersey, with the shock of an earthquake. Emerging from two spacecraft were creatures with tentacles; their mouths were V-shaped. One Martian had a body as large as a bear. All the while scary music increased the tension. At last a voice in the way of an official announcement imparted this news: "Ladies and gentlemen, as incredible as it may seem, both the observations of science and the evidence of our own eyes lead to the inescapable assumption that those strange beings who landed in New Jersey farmlands tonight are the vanguard of an invading army from the planet Mars." So realistic was the show that thousands of listeners became panic-stricken, many evacuating their homes. Orson Welles played the lead voice and directed. In spite of disclaimers, police stations everywhere were taking frantic calls from frightened listeners. No sooner had the broadcast concluded than New Jersey police had invaded Studio 1 at the CBS headquarters, Princeton, New Jersey, their revolvers drawn, until they realized it was just a radio program. All the publicity brought Campbell Soup in as a sponsor, and the *Mercury Theater on the Air* became the *Campbell Playhouse* (December 9, 1938). Welles became an overnight star. The FCC (Federal Communications Commission) ruled no laws had been broken but passed new laws concerning disclaimers and the like.

Name the only actor who was actually married on a live radio show.

On February 12, 1948, Dick Van Dyke, film, television, and Broadway actor, married his childhood sweetheart Marjorie Willetts on *Bride and Groom* (ABC), a thirty-minute radio show that aired weekdays at 2:30 each afternoon from November 26, 1945 to September 15, 1950. The Van Dykes had four children. Dick Van Dyke is thus the only actor to get hitched for real on a radio show.

Name the only composer and lyricist to be accorded a special evening of their musicals broadcast simultaneously on all television networks.

On the night of March 28, 1954, a unique tribute was paid to Rodgers and Hammerstein. Sponsored by General Foods, all the commercial television networks—ABC, NBC, and CBS, plus the old DuMont network—presented ninety minutes of segments from Rodgers and Hammerstein Broadway musicals. Segments featured were from *Oklahoma!, Carousel, State Fair, South Pacific, The King and I,* and other shows by the Broadway masters. Such stars as Jack Benny, Groucho Marx, and Ed Sullivan made the unique evening a memorable tribute and the only time the entire commercial television industry simultaneously devoted time to the same artists to create a grand night for singing.

What is the only town named after a radio or television program?

The only town in the world named after a radio or television program is Truth or Consequences, New Mexico, formerly named Hot Springs. *Truth or Consequences*, on radio from 1935 to 1957 and on television from 1950 to 1958, was a popular game show. In 1950 host and producer Ralph Edwards wondered on television if a town might be willing to change its name to honor the show. Hot Springs' leaders put it to the citizens, who voted to change the town's name; hence Truth or Consequences was born on March 31, 1950.

Can you name the only Rodgers and Hammerstein musical made specifically for television?

The only Rodgers and Hammerstein musical made for television was *Cinderella*, starring Julie Andrews and airing March 31, 1957 on CBS. An audience of 107 million tuned in to enjoy the lavish TV production, the only time a Rodgers and Hammerstein vehicle would be produced specifically for the tube.

Who is the only performer ever fired on live national television?

The only performer fired on television before a national audience was Julius La Rosa, by host Arthur Godfrey on his show *Arthur Godfrey and Friends*. On October 19, 1953, just after La Rosa had completed singing "I'll Take Manhattan," Arthur Godfrey announced before millions, "That, folks, was Julius' swan song." The deluge of calls from around the country almost dismantled the switchboard at CBS, the network that aired the show. It seems that La Rosa, a teen heartthrob, was very much liked. Godfrey later explained to the press that La Rosa had become too arrogant. The fact that he had become so popular and received double the fan mail that Godfrey received grated on Godfrey's nerves. Handled by a big-time agent and blessed with a splendid voice, La Rosa nevertheless went on to have a successful career.

Who is the only member of the Kennedy family to have appeared on a regular television series?

Patricia Kennedy Lawford, sister of President John F. Kennedy, appeared as a regular on a TV sitcom called *Dear Phoebe* on NBC from September 10, 1954, to September 2, 1955. The star of the show was Peter Lawford, to whom she was married from April 24, 1954, to February 1, 1966.

Who is the only prizefighter to lose his life in a fight on national television?

Benny "Kid" Paret had taken numerous blows to the head as administered by his opponent Emile Griffith on February 20, 1961, in a fight carried by ABC's *Fight of the Week*. Paret failed to answer the bell—failed to respond at all after taking a Griffith left jab to the jaw, the blow sending him sinking to the canvas, where death claimed the fallen prizefighter. What was all too bizarre about the incident was ABC's replay of the deathblow, in slow motion no less. ABC got a black eye on this one, with a storm of protests besieging the network's New York headquarters for playing the final sequence over and over again. On September 11, 1964, the curtain descended on ABC's *Fight of the Week*, as sponsors were apparently turned off.

What was the only murder that was seen by millions of eyewitnesses on live television?

The only person murdered before live national television cameras was twenty-four-year-old Lee Harvey Oswald. He was shot on Sunday, November 24, 1963, at 11:30 A.M. while being transferred by Dallas police to the county jail after having been charged with the murder of police officer J. D. Tippit and the murder of President John F. Kennedy. Oswald, a Marine Corps veteran, was being moved through the basement surrounded by press and onlookers when he was approached by Jack Ruby (born Jacob Rubenstein), owner of a local nightclub, the Carousel. Ruby drew a Colt .38, which he habitually carried, shooting Oswald in his left lower chest. Oswald was transferred to Parkland Memorial Hospital and was declared dead at 1:07 P.M. Kennedy had died at the same hospital as Oswald. Oswald was buried at Rosehill Cemetery in Fort Worth, Texas, the only person murdered on live national television.

Name the only horse in film or television to win a Golden Globe Award.

The talking horse on the television sitcom *Mr. Ed* (CBS, 1960-1966) won the Golden Globe Award in 1960. Mr. Ed only talked with Wilbur Post, played by Alan Young, which Post tries to hide from others, resulting in much fun. Mr. Ed was the only Golden Globe winner who was a horse. He was also the only animal with his own Social Security number.

Who is the only children's television host to urge his viewers to steal money?

Soupy Sales was the only television star on live TV-WNEW-TV in New York (Channel 5, now known as Fox 5) to urge his young viewers to steal money from their parents and send it to him. On January 1, 1965, the host of the kiddies' show *The Soupy Sales Children Show* instructed his viewers to go into their parents' wallets and remove "those little pieces of paper with the pictures of George Washington, Benjamin Franklin, and Thomas Jefferson on them and send them to me, and I'll send you a postcard from Puerto Rico." Having received a deluge of U.S. currency from many of his young viewers, Soupy Sales was suspended by WNEW, only to find support from outraged mature viewers, which resulted in Sales's immediate reinstatement. Sales sent the money back to the parents of the children with an apology.

Name the only long-running TV program without a theme song.

Since it was first televised on September 24, 1968, the CBS news show *60 Minutes* has featured not a theme song, but a ticking stopwatch as a soundtrack. The ticking watch is the perfect device to indicate the tension of time passing. Many have said the stopwatch is a star in its own right, along with reporters Mike Wallace, Dan Rather, and Diane Sawyer, to name a few.

Name the only actor to receive three Emmy nominations for playing the same character in three different television shows.

Kelsey Grammer is the only actor to have been nominated three times for an Emmy (supporting actor and leading actor in a comedy series) for three different television shows, for playing the same character, Frasier Crane. Grammer was nominated for his portrayal of Frasier Crane on *Cheers* (1987), a guest appearance on the television show *Wings* (1990), and his own show, *Frasier* (1993). (Note: Grammer won the Best Actor in a Comedy Emmy in 1994, 1995, and 1998.)

Who was the only superhero that appeared in every episode of *Seinfeld*?

Superman was the only superhero who appeared in many different forms in every single episode of the television hit sitcom *Seinfeld*, which ran from 1990 to 1998.

What is the only children's television program to have won dozens of Emmys, more than any other show?

The only children's program to win dozens of Emmys is *Sesame Street*, which has been running for more than thirty years. As of 2003, it has won eighty-five Emmys and is watched by over 125 million people in over 145 countries. It has won more Emmys than any other television show in TV history.

Religion

Name the only book of the Bible in which the name of God is not mentioned?

The Book of Esther is the only book of the Bible in which the name of God is not mentioned. Only 167 verses long, it is about a beautiful Jewish woman who lived in Persia (modern-day Iran) during the fifth century B.C. She foils Haman, an evil minister of the king (Ahasuerus, or Xerxes, her husband) who is plotting to massacre the Jews. The story gave rise to the Jewish holiday of Purim, observed prior to Passover, which celebrates Jewish freedom from Persian persecution. Many biblical historians believe the Book of Esther to be a work of fiction, whose main purpose was to impart hope and courage in the face of adversity.

What is the only religion indigenous to Japan?

The only religion indigenous to Japan is Shinto or Shintoism. Shinto, approximately 3,000 years old, is a religion based on ancient folk belief and rituals. Shinto is a worship of Kami, a concept involving the gods, all aspects of nature, supernatural power, and people. Kami is everywhere and everywhere is Kami. It is a "force" in the universe. Each of the thirteen sects of Shinto has its own founder. There are approximately 30 million people who practice Shinto, most of whom are also Buddhist.

What is the only major religion that wasn't begun by a known prophet?

Hinduism, the most ancient religion known to the world, dating back more than 7,000 years, is the only major religion that wasn't begun by a known prophet. Hinduism is also the only religion in the world which has several million gods all worshipped for different purposes. Hinduism is based on the practice of Dharma, the code of life. There are over 700 million Hindus, mostly in India.

Who was the only one of Christ's twelve apostles to die a natural death?

The only one of the twelve apostles to die a natural death was John. The youngest of the twelve, John is featured sitting to Christ's right in Leonardo da Vinci's *Last Supper*. He stood at the cross with the Virgin Mary and is credited with writing the fourth Gospel. He is believed to have died in his sleep in Asia Minor circa A.D 100. All other eleven apostles died violently via crucifixion, beheading, or stoning.

Name the only soap with a name inspired by a biblical psalm.

The only soap with a name directly inspired by the Bible, specifically Psalm 45, is Ivory soap. Harley Procter of Procter & Gamble, at a Sunday service in 1879, had heard the reading of Psalm 45, "All thy garments smell of myrrh, and aloes, and cassia, out of the ivory palaces, whereby they have made thee glad." Thus Ivory replaced the name of the soap formerly called P & G soap. Ivory is the most widely used soap in the world. It is also the only soap that floats, a phenomenon that was discovered in the mid-1870s at the main plaint in Cincinnati, when by accident tiny air bubbles in one of the processing machines caused the soap to bob in water. When the air bubbles were cleaned from the machine, the soap sank. Now, the process is not only patented but is a carefully guarded secret.

Name the only U.S. state whose number one tourist attraction is of a religious nature.

The only state whose number one tourist attraction is religious in nature is Utah. The tourist attraction is the Mormon Tabernacle (dubbed "the Mormon Vatican"), a large snow-white edifice located in the state capital, Salt Lake City. The state's world-famous Mormon Tabernacle Choir has sold numerous recordings and is renowned for its artistic beauty.

Who is the only woman judge mentioned in the Bible?

Deborah, judge of Israel, is the only woman judge in the Bible. She was also a prophet and military leader known for delivering Israel from the oppression of the Canaanite King Jabin.

In the long line of popes who was the only pontiff assassinated?

On the night of December 16, 882, a German relative poisoned Pope John VIII (872-882), then viciously seized a bludgeon to finish him off. It was a time when little or no protection was given to such esteemed religious (as well as political) figures. Today, with the Vatican a major influence in world affairs, papal security is never taken lightly, and is always being reviewed and upgraded.

Who is **the only woman buried among the popes at the Vatican?**

Sweden's Queen Christina Alexandra (1626-1689), who reigned from 1632 to 1654, is the only woman to be buried among popes at the Vatican. Because of her holiness, she was buried in a tomb at the original St. Peter's Basilica, upon which was built the present-day structure. The site is the burial place of such modern pontiffs as Pope John XXIII, Pope Paul VI, and Pope John Paul I. Christina gave up her throne even though she ruled with laudable zeal. She above all gained a reputation for her charity to the poor. The fact that Christina was a woman in a staunchly male-dominated ecclesiastical institution further enhances this auspicious "only."

Name the only American cleric who was not a bishop to be made a cardinal.

The only American who was not a bishop to be appointed a cardinal of the Roman Catholic Church is the Reverend Avery Dulles, a renowned Jesuit theologian, on January 21, 2001, by Pope John Paul II. Avery Dulles is the son of the former secretary of state under President Eisenhower, John Foster Dulles. While attending Harvard, Avery Dulles began religious studies in theology. A Protestant, he converted to Catholicism while at Harvard. He mentioned how his conversion had shocked both his family and friends, but he called it "the best decision I ever made." After graduating from Harvard as a theologian, Dulles attended Harvard Law School for a brief time before joining the Naval Reserve as an intelligence officer. He won the Croix de Guerre in 1945 for his liaison work with the French navy. A year later he joined the Jesuits and began to train for the priesthood; he was ordained in 1956 by Francis Cardinal Spellman of New York.

Who is the only nun to hold the office of mayor of an American city?

The only nun to hold the office of mayor of an American city was Sister Mary Carolyn of the Sisters of Charity of the Blessed Virgin Mary. She was elected to the office of Mayor of Dubuque, Iowa, in 1980.

What is the only commercial airline to display a religious symbol on its planes?

The only commercial airline to display a religious symbol is Israel's El Al, which displays the Star of David on its fuselage. The flag was created with the Star of David, the Jewish symbol.

Science & Nature

What is the only rock that can be eaten by human beings?

Salt, a naturally formed mineral, which is actually a rock, is the only rock that people can eat. Salt is quite hard when mined and must be processed for the human diet. There are over 14,000 uses for this versatile mineral. It is found in medicine and used as a spice, a preservative, and a cleaning agent; it can be used to extinguish grease fires and to deodorize shoes. Salt ore, also known by its chemical name, sodium chloride, is the only rock eaten by humans.

Name the only animal that can see both infrared and ultraviolet light.

The common goldfish is the only animal that can see infrared and ultraviolet light.

Cite the only marsupial located in North America.

The only marsupial in North America is the common (or Virginia) opossum, which can be found in much of the United States.

Cite the only breed of domestic rabbit that changes color.

The only breed of domestic rabbit that changes color is the Champagne D'Argent; they are born black and change to a dull silver.

Name the only bee that can inflict a sting without disemboweling itself.

The queen bee, whose stinger is not barbed, unlike the stinger of all others of the species, is the only bee that can sting without dying. The queen reserves her stinger for use on other queen bees. Her stinger, being a straight, smooth needle, may be used repeatedly without endangering her life.

Name the only animal besides humans that has been taught to stand on its head.

Circuses would not be caught without at least several elephants that have been taught to stand on their heads, the only animal that does so.

Cite the only bird whose only food consists mostly of leaves.

The hoatzin of South America is the only bird whose main diet is on moist leaves. It does not eat bread.

Name the only continent without ants?

The only continent in the world without any ants is Antarctica. It is also the only continent whose first three letters spell out an insect's name, Ant (arctica).

What is the only milk-producing animal whose milk is naturally homogenized?

The only milk-producing animal (mammal) whose milk is naturally homogenized (of uniform consistency) is the goat. In the case of cows, it is humans with machinery that homogenize the milk.

What the only "barkless" yodeling dog?

The Basenji is the only dog that cannot bark but instead makes a noise that sounds like a yodel; hence it is often called the "yodeling" dog. Found in the Congo, the Basenji has a smooth coat. It is a very prized dog, beloved for its total devotion.

What is the only country where poisonous birds are found?

The only country where poisonous birds are found is Papua New Guinea in the southwest Pacific. The Hooded Pitohui and the Lfrita have feathers that cause blisters on the skin of those who touch them.

Where can one find the only seeds larger than beach balls, the coc de mer or coconut of the sea?

The only place in the world where the seeds of the coc de mer (coconut of the sea) are found is the Seychelles Islands in the Indian Ocean. These seeds are larger than beach balls, some weighing one hundred pounds. They hang in bunches on powerful palm tree branches and are the largest seeds known to man. Often visitors to these islands pay a premium price for just one of the seeds, which are highly prized by the natives, for they are well aware that the seeds are found nowhere else in the world and are believed to bring good fortune to their owners.

Name the only member of the cat family that is actually social by nature.

The only member of the cat family that is actually social is the lion. All others of the species are solitary, including tigers, panthers, jaguars, etc. A group of lions is called a pride. (Note: The males are lazy and treated royally by their female mates.)

Name the only animal whose name changes with the color of its coat.

The only animal with two different names that change with the color of its coat is the weasel. In winter, when the weasel's coat turns white, the animal is properly called the ermine, and in summer, when its coat assumes a reddish brown color, it earns the name of weasel. The only weasels that become ermine live in the north, such as the *Mustela erminea*. The change of the color of the coat is nature's way of protecting the animal by allowing it to blend into its surroundings, making it harder to be seen by both its predators and its prey. Ermine fur has been historically prized, and has been used for kings' robes.

What is the only country where pink elephants actually exist?

The only country in the world where pink elephants can be found is India. The animals wallow in the dried red soil found in some regions, leaving their hide covered with a pink powdery film, which wards off insects and gives the hide a genuine pink pigment.

Name the only breed of dog that actually "hibernates" (passes the cold months or winter in a resting state)?

The raccoon dog, so named because of its similar appearance to a raccoon, is the only dog that hibernates in the winter. The raccoon dog is found in East Asia and Japan and upon close inspection is indeed of the canine family.

Name the only living insect that makes war.

The only living insect that makes war is the ant. Ants plan strategies and take prisoners, which they enslave. The ant is also the only insect that absolutely never sleeps.

What is the only lizard that can make audible sounds?

The only lizard that has a voice is the gecko, a small lizard found chiefly in tropical climates. The gecko is a harmless nocturnal creature.

What is the only mammal with poisonous glands?

The only mammal known to have poisonous glands is the duckbilled platypus. The males have a hollow spur in the heel that is filled with poison.

Cite the only part of the human body that cannot repair itself.

The tooth is the only part of the body that can't repair itself.

What is the only known planet that spins on its side?

Uranus is the only planet that spins on its side; all other planets spin either counterclockwise or clockwise.

Name the only recording that was left on the moon.

The only recording to be left on the moon (on July 20, 1969) for posterity is a gold-plated thirty-three-rpm cast recording of the musical show *Camelot*, which opened on Broadway at the Majestic Theatre on December 3, 1960. It was left on the moon in homage to President John F. Kennedy, who fell in love with the musical.

Where is the only place in the world that accepted a vote from space?

The only place in the world that accepted a vote from space is the state of Texas. It was of course an absentee ballot that was cast from the Russian space station *Mir* (which means 'peace' in Russian) by electronic mail by one of the American astronauts in a local election on November 4, 1997.

Who is the only person to have telephoned the moon?

The only person to have ever telephoned the moon was President Richard M. Nixon, who on July 20, 1969, used a special hookup to speak with Neil Armstrong, Buzz Aldrin, and Michael Collins after the *Apollo 11* moon landing. The president congratulated the trio of astronauts.

Cite the only satellite that has been destroyed by a meteor.

The only satellite destroyed by a meteor was the European Space Agency's *Olympus* in 1993.

What is the only planet in the solar system that does not have a name from Greek or Roman mythology?

Earth is the solar system's only planet whose name is not inspired by Greek or Roman myth. The name derives from the Old English word eorthe.

Sports & the Olympics

Who is the only Rhodes scholar to become a National Basketball Association championship winner and the only pro basketball player to run for President?

Bill Bradley was a Rhodes scholar in 1965 and played with the New York Knicks from 1967 to 1977. He was on the Knicks' NBA championship teams in 1969-70 and 1972-73. After his sports career, Bradley embarked on a political career; he was a senator from New Jersey and a presidential candidate. He stepped aside for Vice President Al Gore in the 2000 campaign.

Name the only sports team ever to perform before a pope, who was the only member of the audience.

In December 1931 the world-famous Harlem Globetrotters played a basketball game before Pope Pius XI. His Holiness never stopped smiling and clapping and laughing as he sat in awe in a special room to view the sports magic for which the Globetrotters had become known and beloved. It would be the only time any basketball team—any sports group—would play before an audience of one: the pope.

What is the only sport that uses a ball whose weight is equal to that of a large feather, or less than an ounce?

A Ping-Pong ball, used in table tennis, is the only ball that is so light. Its regulation weight is .09 ounces, equivalent to 2.5 grams. Golf balls, baseballs, billiard balls, etc., all weigh well over an ounce.

Name the only National Hockey League referee actually blind in one eye to have been approved by the NHL board of governors to ref in the NHL.

William "Bill" Chadwick, called the "greatest" hockey referee the sport has ever known, is the only NHL ref to be blind in one eye. He had instincts second to none and was always a calming, peaceful referee who never let the players get out of hand. Even with vision in only one eye, Chadwick was called upon for playoffs and Stanley Cup games. He did the sport proud with calls right on the money amidst raging hockey sticks, reeling players, and a dizzying puck!

Who was the only son to succeed his father in winning a major golf tournament?

The only son to succeed his father in winning a major golf tournament was Tom Morris. Tom Morris, the father and winner of the 1867 British Open, was succeeded the following year by his son, young Tom Morris, who took the 1868 British Open.

Name the only individual in sports to have been honored with two New York City ticker-tape parades.

Golfing great Bobby Jones, on July 2, 1926, and again on July 2, 1930, was the only individual in sports to have been honored by New York City with two ticker-tape parades. Both parades were held in lower Manhattan's "Canyon of Heroes" to celebrate Jones's victories at the British Open golf tournament.

Name the only female tennis star, and the only female African-American sports figure to be accorded a New York ticker-tape parade.

On July 11, 1957, Althea Gibson, a tennis star from 1950 to 1960, was accorded a ticker-tape parade down lower Manhattan's "Canyon of Heroes," in honor of her Wimbledon (Great Britain) and Forest Hills (U.S. Open) tennis triumphs. She was received at City Hall by Mayor Robert F. Wagner and other New York City officials. Millions of New Yorkers lined city sidewalks while confetti rained down upon the motorcade. Gibson was the rage of tennis in her day and the first African-American female sports figure to win the hearts of Big Apple residents and to be hosted at a luncheon and bestowed with the key to the city.

Name the only gold trophy awarded in the sport of tennis.

The tennis trophy awarded at Wimbledon is almost solid gold. All other tennis trophies, including those for the French, U.S., and Australian Opens, are silver. England's Wimbledon is also the only sports event of any kind to traditionally serve strawberries and cream at concession stands, booths, and dining rooms.

Name the only team and its coach to go to the Super Bowl four years in a row.

The Buffalo Bills (American Football Conference) and their coach, Marv Levy, are the only team and coach to go to the Super Bowl four years in a row. The Bills first went to the Super Bowl in 1991 (Super Bowl XXV). They lost to the New York Giants, 20-19. In 1992 in Super Bowl XXVI they lost to the Washington Redskins, 37-24. In 1993 in Super Bowl XXVII the Bills faced the Dallas Cowboys, losing 52-17, and finally, in 1994 at Super Bowl XXVIII they again lost to the Dallas Cowboys, 30-13. Always a bridesmaid, never a ring.

Name the only football figure to have an automobile named after him.

College football coach Knute Rockne, of Notre Dame, who died in a plane crash in 1931, is the only football figure to have a car named after him. In the year following his death, the Studebaker Corporation produced the Rockne, which retailed for $585. Because of the Great Depression, few consumers could afford the Rockne, and in 1933 the company stopped its production. The Studebaker firm bestowed a gift of the Rockne on Notre Dame. The small South Bend, Indiana, Catholic university had been unknown until Rockne became coach (1918-1931), but winning at football put it on the map as the team that would become known as the Fighting Irish.

Who is the only sports figure in the college football, professional football, and lacrosse halls of fame?

Jim Brown is the only sports figure inducted into the college and professional football halls of fame, as well as into the Lacrosse Hall of Fame. He has been called the greatest running back of all time, with Syracuse University (1953-1956) and with the Cleveland Browns (1957-1965). His 106 rushing touchdowns in the pros is a record that remains unbroken. He rivaled Jim Thorpe in football greatness. At Syracuse University Brown won letters in football, lacrosse, basketball, and track, and was voted All-American in football and lacrosse. He was inducted into the College Football Hall of Fame (South Bend, Indiana) in 1956 and the professional Football Hall of Fame (Canton, Ohio) in 1971, but what makes Jim Brown most unique is his induction into the Lacrosse Hall of Fame in 1956. He is the only college and pro football figure so honored. He went on to become a successful film star and male sex symbol.

Name the only person who was both a college football player and a college coach to be enshrined in the College Football Hall of Fame and the Basketball Hall of Fame.

Amos Alonzo Stagg (1862-1965) was for many years the most successful college gridiron coach with 309 wins (until surpassed by Bear Bryant in 1983). Stagg amassed his enormous number of victories at the University of Chicago, Susquehanna University, and as coach at College of the Pacific . The fact that he was enshrined in the College Football Hall of Fame as a player/coach is an achievement in itself, but in 1959 Stagg became unique when he was inducted into the Basketball Hall of Fame for his effort in promoting the game of basketball at the University of Chicago, working closely with the game's inventor, James Naismith. Stagg, the only player/coach in both the Basketball Hall of Fame and the College Football Hall of Fame, also deserves credit for inventing the tackling dummy, numbers on players' uniforms, and the football huddle.

Name the only college football player to win the "Downtown Athletic Trophy".

The only Heisman Trophy (college football's most prestigious award) that was officially named the Downtown Athletic Trophy was the 1935 trophy won by Jay Berwanger of the University of Chicago, a halfback. In 1936 the award for outstanding collegiate football player was formally changed to its present name.

What are the only two countries to go to war with one another over a soccer game?

The only countries to declare war on one another over a soccer game were El Salvador and Honduras in Central America. Political tensions had been mounting between the two countries, which declared war on July 3, 1969, after El Salvador scored the winning goal on a penalty kick. The score was El Salvador 3, Honduras 2. The game was not even a World Cup title game. The war, which ended less than a week later, became known as the "soccer war."

Who is the only person to have managed four different teams in four different consecutive soccer World Cups?

Bora Milutinovic is the only person to have managed four different teams in four consecutive soccer World Cups: Mexico (1986), Costa Rica (1990), USA (1994), and Nigeria (1998).

Who is the only person to have played both World Cup soccer and World Cup cricket?

The only athlete to have played in World Cup soccer and cricket games is Sir Viv Richards (Isaac Vivian Alexander Richards), who has played soccer for Antigua and cricket for the West Indies.

Name the only Major League Baseball park where fans can observe games by watching from rooftops?

Wrigley Field, Chicago, home of the Chicago Cubs, is the only baseball park where baseball fans can view the entire game from the top of buildings overlooking the park. Prior to each game, fans make arrangements with tenants living in the various apartments to be taken to the roofs, where, for fees ranging from fifty dollars on up, comfortable lawn chairs are provided as well as picnic food, including hot dogs and cold drinks.

Who is the only Major League Baseball player to have hit five hundred home runs or more and to have won over fifty games as a pitcher?

Babe Ruth had over ninety-three pitching wins against forty-four losses while playing with the Boston Red Sox (1914-1919). He also played with the New York Yankees (1920-1933) and closed his career with the Boston Braves (in the National League). As an outfielder (and pitcher) the Babe hit a massive 714 home runs-a record that endured until surpassed by Hank Aaron in 1974.

Name the only time in Major League
Baseball history that a club began the
game with each of its nine members
having the same batting average, .000, lost
the game when the opposing pitcher
no-hit them, and their batting averages
remained the same—no points gained,
no points lost, batting averages still .000.

On opening day, 1940, Bob Feller of the Cleveland Indians pitched a no-hitter against the Chicago White Sox. Since it was opening day, the players of both teams were batting .000. Since the White Sox got no hits and were batting zeros, there were no points to take from them, hence the White Sox averages remained .000. It was the only time in baseball history that happened.

Name the only year and the only Major League Baseball team to have three catchers all on the same team each hit more than twenty home runs.

In 1961 the New York Yankees' Yogi Berra, Elston Howard, and John Blanchard each hit more than twenty home runs. Berra had twenty-two homers, and Blanchard and Howard each hit twenty-one round-trippers.

Who is the only person to have managed the Brooklyn Dodgers, the New York Yankees, and the New York Mets, and to have played with the New York Giants—the only person to have been employed by all four New York major league teams?

Casey Stengel (nicknamed "The Old Professor") is the only person to have been employed by all four New York major league teams. From 1921 through 1923 he played for John McGraw's New York Giants as a right fielder. From 1934 through 1936 Casey managed the Brooklyn Dodgers. From 1949 through 1960 he managed the New York Yankees, taking the team to many World Series victories. Last, he managed the New York Mets from 1962 through 1965, making Stengel the only baseball player to been employed by all major league teams that have played in New York.

Name the only major leaguer to hit a home run in a foreign country that won a baseball World Series.

On October 23, 1993, in the bottom of the ninth inning of game six of the World Series in Toronto, Joe Carter hit a home run off Mitch Williams of the Philadelphia Phillies to win the 1993 World Series for the Toronto Blue Jays. The score was 8-6. It was and remains the only home run hit outside the United States that would win a World Series. Joe Carter is the only player to earn such a distinction.

What Major League Baseball player used the only known six-finger glove? Where can that glove be found today?

The only six-finger baseball glove is now displayed in the Baseball Hall of Fame at Cooperstown in upstate New York. The six-finger mitt belonged to pitcher Greg Harris, who toiled for the Montreal Expos (National League). Harris was ambidextrous and thus on September 25, 1995, used the glove, specially designed for him with its six fingers to fit on his right and left hands, to retire several Cincinnati Reds batters. There are no rules in the major league rule book governing the number of fingers on a glove. Today the Greg Harris six-finger baseball glove for both left and right hands is enshrined at Cooperstown.

Name the only major league baseball player to hit into a triple play and hit a grand slam home run in the same game.

On August 6, 2001, Boston Red Sox Scott Hatteberg hit into a triple play—banging a line drive to Texas Rangers shortstop Alex Rodriguez, who caught the ball and flipped it to his second baseman, who stepped on the bag for the second out. As he caught the runner off the bag, he tagged him before he could get back to first base—three outs in one play, a triple play. Hatteberg would come up to bat later in the game with the bases loaded, hitting a grand slam home run. It is the only time in baseball history that a player hit into a triple play and also hit a grand slam home run—all in the same game. The Red Sox won the game, 10-7.

Who is the only man to play in both a Masters golf tournament and a World Series?

The only man to play in both the Masters and the World Series was Sam Byrd, who played in the 1932 World Series for the New York Yankees—the Bronx Bombers—when they swept the Chicago Cubs four games to zero. The Series was famous for Babe Ruth having pointed to the place where he would hit a home run, which he did. Byrd later played in the Masters, in 1941 and 1942.

Who is the only U.S. federal judge in the Baseball Hall of Fame?

The only U.S. federal judge in the Baseball Hall of Fame is Judge Kenesaw Mountain Landis, baseball's first commissioner from 1921 to 1944. Landis, U.S. district judge in Illinois, presided over the breakup of oil giant Standard Oil and other vital litigation, imposing hefty fines and stiff sentences in some cases. In 1920, Major League Baseball was embroiled in a scandal—players were believed to have gambled on the 1919 World Series, in which the White Sox played the Cincinnati Reds. The players were acquitted, but Landis nevertheless barred all those involved—eight in all, including "Shoeless" Joe Jackson—from baseball for life. Landis was credited with restoring the good and honorable name of big league baseball. On June 12, 1939, Landis gave the dedicatory address officially opening the Baseball Hall of Fame at Cooperstown in upstate New York. Five years later, in 1944, Judge Kenesaw Mountain Landis was enshrined in the Baseball Hall of Fame, the only federal court judge to be so honored. In the year Landis was enshrined he was the only inductee.

Name the only major league umpire to call a World Series no-hitter.

The only umpire to call a World Series no-hitter, a perfect game, was Babe Pinelli, who on October 8, 1956, umpired game five of the Series at Yankee Stadium when Don Larsen threw a no-hit perfect game. Pinelli called Dale Mitchell out on strikes, the twenty-seventh batter to face Larsen of the New York Yankees; Larsen was pitching against the Brooklyn Dodgers' Sal Maglie. Pinelli was the crew chief of the six umpires, and he had tears in his eyes after Larsen threw the last pitch of the game. Yogi Berra was the catcher. Babe Pinelli's uniform was enshrined in the Hall of Fame at Cooperstown, New York. Of course Pinelli, who died in 1984, said it was his greatest game, having been an umpire since 1935. The game was his last umpired behind the plate, as Babe retired after the 1956 World Series.

Who is the only Olympian to have been accorded a New York City ticker-tape parade?

The only Olympian to be accorded a New York City ticker-tape parade was Jesse Owens on August 29, 1936, only days after triumphing at the Berlin Olympics in track and field. While Owens was waving to the masses, an extraordinary thing happened: a brown paper bag that Owens thought contained a sandwich was tossed up to him from someone in the crowd. Resting the bag on the automobile seat, Owens eventually shoved it into his side jacket pocket. At the hotel, feeling famished and unable to wait for an evening banquet, Jesse remembered the paper bag. He believed he would find a nice sandwich inside. When opening the bag, however, he discovered not a sandwich but $10,000 in $100 bills!

Cite the only Olympics that included the shooting of animals as one of the events for which gold, silver, and bronze medals were awarded.

At the 1900 Olympics the shooting of live doves (pigeons) was on the bill. Belgium's Leon de Lunden took the gold. Using a Winchester 73, the marksman brought down twenty-one birds as they were in flight. The event met with protests, particularly when the second-place silver medalist shot twenty birds. Sports lovers for the most part found little to cheer about. The Olympic authorities were reminded that the deliberate killing of animals went against the principles and ideals of the Olympics: peace and brotherhood between nations. The dove is the symbol of peace. The harming of animals had seen its last and only Olympics, for the event was dropped permanently thereafter.

Who is the only two-time Olympic decathlon winner?

The only two-time Olympic decathlon winner—a ten-event affair—is Bob Mathias. In London, England, at the 1948 Olympics, Mathias excelled in the big ten-100 meters, 400 meters, high jump, shot put, broad jump, 110-meter hurdles, discus throw, pole vault, javelin throw, and the 1,500 meters. Four years later, in 1952 at Helsinki, Finland, Mathias repeated his decathlon achievement and went on to become the only person to twice win the Olympic decathlon.

Name the only athlete to possess an Olympic gold medal and a Super Bowl ring.

Bob "Bullet" Hayes won an Olympic gold medal in Tokyo in 1964 in the 100-meter dash; he was called the "Fastest Human Being in the World." In 1965 Hayes joined the Dallas Cowboys as a wide receiver, winning a Super Bowl ring in 1972-Dallas Cowboys 24, Miami Dolphins 3. Bob "Bullet" Hayes—one of the fastest men in the NFL and the only Super Bowl ring and Olympic gold medal holder—passed away at age fifty-nine of cancer on September 18, 2002.

Cite the only country not to win a gold medal at the Summer Olympic Games while it was the host country.

Canada is the only while it was the host country not to have won a gold medal in the Summer Olympics. It hosted the Summer Olympic Games in 1976.

Name the only U.S. athlete to ignore the U.S. boycott of the Winter Olympics in Moscow in 1980.

The only American athlete to ignore the U.S. boycott of the Winter Olympics in Moscow (1980) was runner Willie Davenport who had won the gold in 1968. Davenport participated in the bobsled competition, but did not win. He was an African American who won numerous plaudits from his Soviet hosts for following his passion and deep-sixing politics.

U.S.
Presidents

Who was the only president never to have resided in the White House?

George Washington (1789-1797) was the only president to never live in the White House. Although he oversaw the construction of the building, his successor, the nation's second president, John Adams (1797-1801), was the first president to reside there.

Name the only first lady who donated silverware and other prized silver objects to be minted into American coins.

Martha Washington is the only First Lady who donated precious objects to be minted into American coins. In 1792 her husband, President George Washington, entreated her to donate prized silver objects, including silverware, to be melted down into American coins—silver five-cent pieces—with the establishment of the Philadelphia mint, as sanctioned by Congress the previous year. Martha Washington thus became the only First Lady who contributed her own treasure toward the creation of a U.S. currency, a silver five-cent piece.

Name the only vice president to have killed another person (other than in wartime).

The only vice president to kill another person was Aaron Burr, vice president to Thomas Jefferson from 1801 to 1805. Burr fled after killing Secretary of the Treasury Alexander Hamilton in a gun duel which took place July 11, 1804, while he was still vice president. Burr did not remain as vice president for Jefferson's second term, and in 1807 was brought up on an unrelated charge of treason; he was acquitted.

Name the only U.S. president whose death went unnoticed.

The only former U.S. president whose death went unnoticed—no flags flown at half-staff, no proclamations, etc.—was John Tyler, president from 1841 to 1845. The reasons: the United States was embroiled in the Civil War from 1861 to 1865, and Tyler died in Richmond, Virginia, in the South, on January 18, 1862.

Who was the only president to have earned a patent?

Abraham Lincoln, who had a repuation for being fascinated by mechanical processes, was the only president to earn a patent. On May 22, 1849, Lincoln received Patent No. 6469 for a device to lift boats over shoals. Lincoln's invention was never manufactured.

Name the only U.S. vice president never to have served at that post.

The only vice president never to serve was William R. King, the running mate of Franklin Pierce (1853-1857), fourteenth U.S. president. Vice President King was ill with tuberculosis in Cuba at the time of Pierce's election. By a special act of Congress, King was permitted to take the oath of office in Cuba. Returning to the United States, King died only days later at his Alabama estate, never having served a day in office.

Name the only U.S. president to have been an ordained minister.

President James A. Garfield, the twentieth president of the United States, was a minister in the Church of the Disciples of Christ at the time of his election. He was assassinated on July 12, 1881.

Who is the only U.S. president to have undergone an operation at sea?

President Grover Cleveland was the only U.S. president to have an operation at sea. On July 1, 1893, he had a cancerous growth removed from his mouth, necessitating removal of his upper left jaw and its replacement with an artificial one, while aboard the vessel *Oneida* in Long Island Sound.

Who is the only U.S. president to have been born on an American national holiday?

Calvin Coolidge was born on July 4, 1872. He served as president from 1923 to 1929.

Name the only person to win the nomination for U.S. president from a major political party, run for the presidency three times, and never win.

The only man nominated three times to run for U.S. president by a major party, the Democrats, who lost all three times, was William Jennings Bryan, who in 1896 and 1900 ran on the Democratic ticket against Republican candidate William McKinley and was defeated both times. In 1908 Bryan ran as a Democrat against William Howard Taft and lost his third and final quest for the U.S. presidency. It is interesting to note that all three presidential candidates had the same first name, William. Bryan is more popularly remembered as being one of the prosecuting attorneys in the Scopes trial in 1925, which focused on Charles Darwin's theory of evolution.

Who is the only U.S. president to be awarded the Congressional Medal of Honor?

· The only U.S. president to be awarded the Congressional Medal of Honor was Theodore Roosevelt, for his heroism in the Spanish-American War (1898). Teddy was remembered as the leader of the Rough Riders Regiment, which fought victoriously in a confrontation known as the Battle of San Juan Hill in Cuba. The posthumous award, long overdue, was bestowed by President Bill Clinton on January 20, 2001.

Name the only president to weigh over three hundred pounds on his inauguration day.

William Howard Taft, twenty-seventh president (1909-1913), weighed over three hundred pounds.Taft was so heavy that he once got stuck inside the White House bathtub. His wife—Helen Herron Taft—tried to pull him out, but failed. She had to call the White House carpenters to smash open the tub. A special bathtub that could hold up to four average-sized men was then installed.

Who is the only president to have raised sheep on the White House lawn?

Woodrow Wilson, president from 1913-1921, was famous for raising sheep on the White House lawn. Their wool was sold to raise money for the Red Cross in World War I. The grazing sheep also cut groundskeeping costs, a benefit for the war effort.

Name the only U.S. president whose likeness appeared on a coin while he was in office.

The only U.S. president whose image appeared on a coin while he was serving as president was Calvin Coolidge. The coin, a half-dollar piece, commemorated the U.S. sesquicentennial on July 4, 1926, while Coolidge was president. The fact that the image of George Washington also appeared on the coin, in profile with Coolidge, makes the coin the only one minted by the United States that depicts two presidents. The coin was withdrawn from circulation after the sesquicentennial.

Name the only U.S. president to drop out of law school, yet take the bar exam and pass.

Franklin D. Roosevelt, thirty-second president of the United States (1933-1945), dropped out of law school but passed the bar. While Roosevelt was at Columbia University in 1905 he complained that law school was interfering with his social life. That same year he married Eleanor. Still wishing to pursue a vital political career, law being the most ideal conduit to the presidency, Roosevelt managed to take the New York State Bar Examination—and passed by the skin of his teeth.

Name the only U.S. president to have won the presidency for four consecutive terms.

Franklin D. Roosevelt served as U.S. president—number thirty-two—from 1933 until his sudden death, on April 12, 1945, a total of just over twelve years. FDR's terms began in 1933, 1937, 1941, and 1945. He was the only president to have won the presidency four times.

Who was the only president to have taken the oath of office on an airplane?

Upon the assassination of President John F. Kennedy on November 22, 1963, Vice President Lyndon Baines Johnson took the oath of office to become the thirty-sixth U.S. president. The ceremony took place aboard Air Force One. The deceased president's widow, Jacqueline Kennedy, witnessed the swearing in of the new president, as did President Johnson's spouse, the new first lady, Lady Bird Johnson. Thus President Lyndon B. Johnson remains the only U.S. president to be sworn in to the office on an airplane—Air Force One.

Who was the only president and vice president to resign from their positions?

The only president to resign was Richard Nixon, as a result of the Watergate affair in 1974. The only vice president to resign from his position was Spiro T. Agnew, vice president to President Richard M. Nixon. Agnew resigned October 10, 1973, pleading no contest to charges of income tax evasion while he was governor of Maryland.

Who is the only president who took the option to "affirm" rather than "swear" to uphold the Constitution?

For religious reasons, Franklin Pierce at his inauguration in 1853 "affirmed" rather than "sweared" to uphold the Constitution. Pierce was Episcopalian.

Name the only future U.S. president and first lady who starred in a feature film together. What was the film?

The film stars were Ronald Reagan and his wife Nancy Davis. He was the future president of the United States, and Davis, who was to become Nancy Reagan, the future First Lady. The film was the 1957 movie *Hellcats of the Navy*.

Cite the only record album about the first family ever recorded. Which first family?

The only record album about the first family was a comedy album by Vaughn Meader entitled *The First Family*, issued in 1962 by Cadence Records. The album was about President John F. Kennedy and his family. It sold about four and a half million copies. The album was still in high sales orbit when JFK was assassinated in Dallas in 1963, and sales then plummeted. Eventually, out of respect for Mrs. Kennedy, the record firm withdrew existing albums from stores. As destiny would have it, a collectors' frenzy immediately took hold, and the remaining copies were soon gobbled up.

Name the only airport to be named after a living U.S. president?

Located in Washington, D.C., Reagan National Airport is the only airport named after a living president. It is named after President Ronald Reagan, who was the fortieth president of the United States, from 1981 to 1989.

Name the only U.S. president to serve as U.S. ambassador to the United Nations and director of the Central Intelligence Agency (CIA).

George Bush, who was president from 1989-1993, is the only U.S. president to have served as ambassador to the United Nations—from 1971 through 1972. Bush is also the only president to have served as director of the CIA, from 1976 to 1977.

Name the only U.S. president to have twin daughters.

Barbara and Jenna Bush, fraternal twins, were born to George W. Bush and Laura Bush on November 25, 1981. George W. Bush is the only U.S. president to have twin daughters.

Encore

Name the only person to have been married to a Most Valuable Player (MVP) in baseball and then to a Pulitzer Prize winner.

Marilyn Monroe is the only person to have had two such spouses. On January 14, 1954, she married former New York Yankees center fielder Joe DiMaggio, the three-time most valuable player (MVP in 1939, 1941, and 1947). They were divorced that same year, on October 27, 1954. On June 29, 1956, Monroe married playwright Arthur Miller, who in 1949 won a Pulitzer Prize (and Tony Award) for his play *Death of a Salesman*, and in 1955 won a Pulitzer for *A View from the Bridge*. The couple was divorced on January 24, 1961. Monroe died in Hollywood on August 4, 1962, the only person to have been married to a Pulitzer Prize winner and a baseball MVP.

Name Elvis Presley's only concert album in which there is no singing.

Having Fun with Elvis on Stage (RCA), released in October 1974, is Elvis's only concert album in which there is no singing. It reached number thirty on Billboard's Hot LP Chart and consists entirely of dialogue taken from "The King's" previous concerts. One can hear Elvis chatting with audiences in between songs. The album was originally marketed only at Presley's live concerts.

What is the only U.S. black college founded by a white man?

The only U.S. black college founded by a white man is Howard University in Washington, D.C. It was founded in 1867 by Civil War Union general Oliver O. Howard, who sought to improve the lot of "Negroes" through education. Howard University has always accepted people of all skin colors.

Who is the only woman to survive a barrel dive into Niagara Falls?

The only woman known to survive a barrel dive into Niagara Falls was Anna Edison Taylor. On October 24, 1901, Taylor made her successful barrel roll over the falls before a crowd of more than four thousand witnesses. Within an hour after disappearing into the profusion of rushing water, Taylor, tightly secured in her oak barrel, was unfettered. She was slightly unconscious with a bleeding head wound, but would live for many years afterward to tell her story.

Who is the only person to win fame for a wax museum that housed her creations?

The only person ever to become known universally for a wax museum and wax creations was Swiss wax modeler Marie Tussaud (1760-1850). Tussaud's Wax Museum (officially named Madame Tussaud's Exhibitions) was originally located on Baker Street, London, England (now on Marylebone Road). Having been closely associated with Louis XVI and Marie Antoinette, king and queen of France (1774-1793), Tussaud was a French tutor to their children and ended up in prison during the French Revolution (1789-1793). While in prison Tussaud created wax replicas of the guillotined heads brought to her cell daily and dumped before her from a cloth bag. Somehow, Tussaud's life was spared. In 1803 she moved her thriving wax business to England, where she created her renowned wax figures and, of greatest interest, a "Chamber of Horrors," featuring wax figures of criminals. Tussaud also produced wax instruments of torture as well as the heads of famous and infamous people. Today, more than a century after her death, Madame Tussaud's Wax Museum is still in existence, and figures of our time—Hitler, U.S. presidents, etc.—are immortalized there in wax. (Note: Most recently, wax museums bearing the Tussaud name have opened in other parts of the world, for example, in New York City.)

Name the only person to own his own private subway car.

The only private subway car in the world was owned by August Belmont, Jr., who also owned Belmont Racetrack in New York and was the financier of New York's first subway, the Interborough Rapid Transit Co. (IRT). Belmont reasoned that since every tycoon had a private railroad car, why shouldn't he have a private subway car? Belmont named his private car the *Mineola*. Completed in 1904, Belmont's *Mineola* was no ordinary subway car, as one might board today, but instead a crowning jewel of elegance. It had crystal chandeliers, a lounge designed for maximum comfort, and a kitchenette or galley, where only the finest food was served, accompanied by the best brandies, coffees, and teas, as well as cooling summer drinks.

Who is the only U.S. Supreme Court justice to wear gold bands on the sleeves of his robes?

Chief Justice of the U.S. Supreme Court William Rehnquist is the only U.S. Supreme Court justice to wear gold bands on the sleeves of his robes. The gold bands on his flowing sleeves were designed by Rehnquist himself: four gold bands, two on each sleeve, called by some court watchers "Rehnquist's flight of whimsy."

Name the only person to have climbed the World Trade Center.

George H. Willig, nicknamed "the Human Fly," is the only person to have climbed New York City's World Trade Center. At 6:30 A.M. on May 26, 1977, using self-made climbing devices, he scaled the South Tower of the World Trade Center—all 110 floors—to the astonishment of stunned passersby and the police. Thousands observed breathlessly as Willig became smaller and smaller from their vantage point on the street below. It took Willig three and a half hours to perform the feat. The next day charges were brought against him by the City of New York, and a fine of $250,000 was imposed. In the end the city dropped the charges and fined Willig $110, or $1 for each floor, and received a promise from "the Human Fly" never to scale any city edifice again.

Name the only "luxury" ocean liner owned by the United States and funded in part with taxpayers' dollars.

The largest merchant ship ever built by the United States, the SS *United States*, launched on her maiden voyage July 3, 1952, is the only luxury liner funded in part with taxpayers' dollars. She would compete with such luxury vessels as the *Queen Mary* and *Queen Elizabeth's I* and *II*. Built at a cost of $73 million, the SS *United States* contained huge 240,000-horsepower steam turbines enabling her to move at fifty miles per hour. In her day the SS *United States* had no equals, and was considered all around to have been the best ocean liner ever built.

What is the only luxury ocean liner to be rammed by another vessel?

The only luxury ocean liner to be rammed by another vessel was the *Andrea Doria*, named after the Italian admiral Andrea Doria Alsoa, a statesman who lived from 1466 to 1560. On July 26, 1956, the beautiful luxury liner, the pride of Italy, sank sixty miles off Nantucket Island, Massachusetts, after being rammed by the icebreaker *Stockholm*.

Where can you find the only
light bulb that has been burning continuously
for one hundred years?

The only light bulb in the world to have burned continuously for one hundred years can be found at Livermore Fire Department's Station Number 6 in Livermore, California. The hand-blown pear-shaped bulb is a three-watt night-light, whose soft roselike incandescence offers a precious sense of warmth and nostalgia. The Shelby Electric Company donated it to the firehouse in 1901 when the owner sold the business. To authenticate the fact that the bulb has been burning for a miraculous one hundred years, experts from General Electric were brought to the firehouse to perform tests with delicate instruments. To ensure that the light bulb continues to burn for another one hundred years, it functions on the backup generator used by the fire station. On June 8, 2001, the town of Livermore paid homage to their unusual celebrity with a festival, a fund-raiser for charity where prizes were awarded. It was the only charitable fund-raiser and festival to have honored a light bulb!

Cite the only dog that can get gout.

The only dog that can get gout is the Dalmatian.

Name the only national flag that is flown differently during times of peace and war.

The flag of the Philippines is the only national flag that is flown differently during times of peace and war. The blue portion of the flag is flown on top in times of peace and the red portion is flown on top during times of war.

Name the only king without a mustache in a pack of cards.

The only king in a pack of cards without a mustache is the king of hearts.

What is the only U.S. state capital that does not have a McDonald's?

Montpelier, Vermont, is the only U.S. state capital that does not have a McDonald's.

What is the only McDonald's in the world that has teal arches instead of golden arches?

The only McDonald's in the world that has teal arches is one located in Sedona, Arizona, so that the building would not clash with the area's landscape.

Name the only actress to have three presidents (future and past) serve as pallbearers at her funeral.

In 1965, at the funeral of the movie star Jeanette MacDonald, former presidents Dwight D. Eisenhower and Harry S Truman, along with future president Ronald Reagan, served as pallbearers for the beautiful and talented actress.

Name the only coin to have fetched more than $3 million at an auction, the only coin of its kind that survived destruction.

The coin is a 1933 $20 double-eagle gold piece, which survived being recalled and melted down as part of President Franklin Delano Roosevelt's U.S. currency gold recall. The coin ended up in the coin collection of an Egyptian prince and was recovered by the FBI. In August 2002 the U.S. treasury sold the 1933 $20 double-eagle to a private collector for more than $3 million, the most ever paid for a coin at an auction.

What and where is the the only painting by Leonardo da Vinci on permanent display in the United States?

The only original painting by da Vinci on permanent display hangs in the National Gallery in Washington, D.C. It's a portrait of Ginevra di Benci, the wife of a politician in Florence.

Name the only player in baseball history to be on four World Series championship teams in his first four seasons in the majors.

Joe DiMaggio (New York Yankees) remains the only player in baseball history to be on four World Series championship teams (1936-1939) during his first four seasons in the majors.

What is the only city in which all major sports teams have the same colors?

Pittsburgh is the only city in which all major sports teams have the same colors—black and gold.

Name the only actor to have owned all of the films in which he starred.

The "King of Daredevil Comedy," Harold Lloyd remains the only actor to have owned all of the films that he ever starred in. Lloyd gained fame as "Lonesome Luke," and for his creation of the bespectacled character simply named Harold.

What is the only animated feature film to be nominated for the best picture Academy Award?

Disney's *Beauty and the Beast* (1992) is the only animated feature film to have ever been nominated for the best picture Academy Award. *Beauty and the Beast* is a heartwarming film about a beautiful young girl named Belle (voice provided by Paige O'Hara) who becomes weary of her life in a small, provincial town. Elsewhere, a fairy places a prince under a spell of ugliness because of his inability to show love or compassion. The prince would remain the Beast until a kindhearted woman falls in love with him. The film *Beauty and the Beast* is a beautiful retelling of this age-old classic, with enchanting songs and captivating animation.

Name the only actor to have played both Jesus Christ and Satan.

Max von Sydow is the only actor to have played Jesus Christ and Satan. Von Sydow played Jesus Christ in the film *The Greatest Story Ever Told* (1965) and later played Satan in *Needful Things* (1993).

Name the only ventriloquist to receive an Oscar.

Edgar Bergen was accorded an Oscar in 1937—a special Oscar for the creation of his ventriloquist dummy, Charlie McCarthy. Together ventriloquist-actor Bergen and sidekick Charlie appeared in numerous films, including *The Goldwyn Follies* and *Charlie McCarthy Detective*. Bergen's other dummy was Mortimer Snerd. Actress Candice Bergen, his daughter, was oft heard to fret that Dad gave more affection to Charlie McCarthy than to her.

Index

A

B

Babe Ruth (set home run and pitching records), 198

"Ballad of the Green Berets, The" (written by a Green Beret, topped *Billboard* chart), 79

BASEBALL

Babe Pinelli (umpire) called World Series no-hitter, 206

Babe Ruth set home run and pitching records, 198

Casey Stengel employed by all four New York major league teams, 201

1940 game where batting averages began and ended at .000, 199

Greg Harris wore six-fingered glove, 203

Joe Carter hit home run in foreign country that won World Series, 202

Joe DiMaggio on four World Series championship teams in first four seasons, 240

Judge Kenesaw Mountain Landis only U.S. federal judge in Hall of Fame, 205

Sam Byrd played in both Masters golf tournament and World Series, 204

Scott Hatteberg hit into a triple play and hit a grand slam home run in same game, 204

Wrigley Field only park where games can be viewed free from nearby rooftops, 197

Yankees (in 1961) had three catchers each hit over 20 home runs, 200

Basenji (barkless yodeling dog), 174

Beach City, Ohio (not a beach in sight), 36

BEATLES

"Martha My Dear" named after Paul McCartney's dog, 140

Paul McCartney songs banned by BBC in 1972, 142

Beauty and the Beast (only animated feature film nominated for best picture Academy Award), 242

Bees (queen can sting without disemboweling herself), 171

Behind the Great Wall (only film to use Aroma-Rama), 99

Belize (jaguar preserve), 18

Bellow, Saul (received three National Book Awards), 62

Belmont, August Jr. (owned private subway car), 232

BEN-HUR

only biblical movie to win best picture Oscar, 120

written by U.S. general and filmed twice, 90

Bergen, Edgar (only ventriloquist to get an Oscar), 243

BERLIN, IRVING

only American composer and lyricist to live past 100th birthday, 143

wrote four songs with titles that became film titles, 136

Berwanger, Jay (won Downtown Athletic Trophy), 195

Birds, poisonous (Papua New Guinea), 174

Bledowska Desert (only true desert in Europe), 16

Boleyn, Ann (only six-fingered British royal figure), 42

Bolivia (only South American country with two capitals), 15

Bond, James (married in film *On Her Majesty's Secret Service*), 106

Boston (rhymes with Austin, Texas), 37

Bradley, Bill (Rhodes scholar, NBA champ, presidential candidate), 185

Brando, Marlon (nominated for Oscar four years in a row), 117

BRAZIL

named after tree, 9

rhinoceros voted to city council, 27

BRITISH ROYALTY

Boleyn, Ann (wife of Henry VIII; only six-fingered British royal figure), 42

Edward VIII and Wallis Simpson, record price paid for wedding cake, 50

Luxembourg, 24

Nepal, 22, 57

Nicaragua, 9

Panama, 11

Papua New Guinea, 174

Poland, 16

Russia, 11

Rwanda, 21

Samoa, 80

Switzerland, 22, 75

Turkey, 52

United States, 20, 51, 54-55

Vatican, 76

Vatican City, 14, 24, 28

Vienna, Austria, 113

Curie, Marie, and Irène Joliot-Curie (only mother and daughter to win Nobel Prize individually), 48

Custer, General George Armstrong (brought wife and pets into military camp in wartime), 78

Cyprus (map of country on flag), 23

D

Dalmation only dog that can get gout, 237

Damon, Matt (won Oscar for best screenplay in film in which he also appeared), 127

Dance, 72-73

Davenport, Willie (only American athlete at 1980 Moscow Winter Olympics), 211

Dead Sea (one can't swim in), 10

Dean, James (Rebel Without a Cause only film he starred in and was not nominated for Oscar), 118

Deborah (only woman judge in the Bible), 164

DECLARATION OF INDEPENDENCE

signed by clergyman (John Witherspoon), 46

signed by siblings (Lee brothers), 45

DESERTS

Lebanon only Middle Eastern country without a desert, 16

Poland has only desert in Europe, 16

Dial M for Murder (only Hitchcock film filmed in 3-D), 102

Diamond mine (only U.S. mine in Arkansas), 30

Diego Garcia (has only U.S. air base not found in a country), 87

Dietrich, Marlene (usher at a film premiere), 98

DiMaggio, Joe (on four World Series championship teams in first four seasons), 240

Dipendra (named king of Nepal despite being brain dead), 57

DOGS

basenji, a barkless yodeling dog, 174

dalmation only dog that can get gout, 237

"Martha My Dear" named after Paul McCartney's dog, 140

raccoon dog hibernates in winter, 178

Donovan, William "Wild Bill" (much-decorated soldier), 84

Doolittle, Jimmy (penetrated "sacred" Japanese airspace in World War II), 53

Drury Lane Theatre (contributed stage-prop rifles to World War II), 66

Dulles, Rev. Avery (became cardinal without being bishop), 166

Dunn, Michael (only dwarf to be nominated for both Academy Award and Tony Award), 123

Durante, Jimmy (had nose insured), 105

E

Earth (name not from Greek or Roman mythology), 183

EDWARD VIII

lost crown because of liaison with Wallis Simpson, 49

record price paid for cake from wedding to Wallis Simpson, 50

EGYPT, ANCIENT

Cleopatra VII only Ptolemaic family member to speak Egyptian rather than Greek, 39

female pharaoh (Hatshepsut), 39

El Al (religious symbol on planes), 167

Elkader (named after Islamic revolutionary), 32

Eleanor, Queen of Aquitaine (sat on both French and British thrones), 41

ELEPHANTS

only animal to stand on head, 172

pink ones found in India, 178

Elizabeth I (reigned but never married), 43

EL SALVADOR

does not border Caribbean, 11

went to war with Honduras over soccer game, 195

Epstein brothers (Julius and Philip) received Oscars for same film (*Casablanca*), 116

Equator (Congo River flows on both sides of), 13

Eskimos (subject matter of opera *Kaddara*), 130

Esther, Book of (only book of Bible in which God is not mentioned), 159

F

Finland (only World War II Axis nation not declared war on by United States), 52

Finnish street signs and TV broadcasts (Negaunee, Michigan), 33

Fiske, William M. III (only U.S. soldier buried at St. Paul's Cathedral in London), 83

FLAGS

map of country on (Cyprus), 23

pair of triangular pennants (Nepal), 22

single color (Libya), 21

single letter on (Rwanda), 21

square (Switzerland), 22

Texas flag flies at same height as U.S. flag, 29

Florida (state motto same as on U.S. coins), 34

Fonteyn, Margot (given title "prima ballerina assoulta"), 72

Ford, John (only director to win four Oscars), 115

Forever and a Day (directed by seven people), 95

Frank, Anne (diary became Broadway play and won Pulitzer Prize and Tony Award), 65

Frayn, Michael (competed with wife for Whitbread prize), 69

G

Gardner, Ava (buried in same manner as in her film *The Barefoot Contessa*), 106

Garfield, James A. (president and ordained minister), 216

Gecko (lizard that makes sounds), 179

Genevieve (score rather than composer nominated for Oscar), 110

GERMANY

Turkey only Middle Eastern country to sign friendship pact with Nazis, 52

United States only country officially declared war on during World War II, 51

Gibraltar (Rock-English spoken), 12

Gibson, Althea (ticker-tape parade), 189

Goat (produces naturally homogenized milk), 173

Godfrey, Arthur (fired Julius La Rosa on live TV), 151

Goldfish (sees infrared and ultraviolet light), 170

Gone with the Wind fined for using word "damn," 93

Grammer, Kelsey (received three Emmy nominations for playing same character in three different TV shows), 156

GREAT BRITAIN

no country name on postage stamps, 12

royalty. See British royalty

Guinness, Sir Alec (played Hitler), 96

H

Halaby, Lisa (only American to become queen of Islamic nation), 56

Hamlisch, Marvin (got three Oscars same year), 112

U

V

W